Women in Management

Career Development for Managerial Success

CARY L. COOPER B.S., M.B.A., M.SC., PH.D., F.B.PS.S.
Professor of Organizational Psychology
University of Manchester

MARILYN J. DAVIDSON B.A., M.A., PH.D.
Research Fellow
UMIST

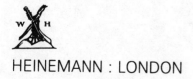

HEINEMANN : LONDON

William Heinemann Ltd
10 Upper Grosvenor Street, London W1X 9PA

LONDON   MELBOURNE   TORONTO   JOHANNESBURG   AUCKLAND

© Cary L. Cooper and Marilyn J. Davidson 1984
First published 1984

Cooper, Gary L.
  Women in management.
  1. Women executives
  I. Title   II. Davidson, Marilyn J.
  658.4′2   HF5500.2

ISBN 0–434–90262–4

Typeset by Deltatype, Ellesmere Port
Printed and bound in Great Britain by
Biddles Ltd, Guildford and King's Lynn

Contents

Foreword

'I see no reason why women can't do top jobs. But you can't expect a young woman to be able to join an organization and say, "I want a career which will give me a chance to be Director-General and will give me a chance to have one baby or more and expect to come back and continue like a man . . .". It would be grossly unfair to the organization and to males' (senior BBC male manager, *Women in Top Jobs 1968–1979*, published by Heinemann).

The above quotation is the crux of the problem facing the majority of women who wish to pursue a career. Women are expected to fulfill their biological role but at the same time if they choose to follow a career they are expected to accept the same terms as their male colleagues. The difference is, of course, that their male colleagues can have one, two, or even more babies without it breaking their career pattern. It is quite remarkable that this attitude should prevail at a time when 62 per cent of all married women between the ages of 16 and 59 are at work and at a time when the so-called traditional family, composed of a bread-winning father, a dependant wife at home and two children, constitutes only 5 per cent of families in the U.K.

Women are still thought of in their family roles and men in their work and business roles. This was very apparent in the Recommendations of Franks' Report in 1963 which led to the establishment of Manchester Business School and London Business School. Here we saw the male image par excellence. Only once in the Report, and that in passing, were women ever mentioned. The whole image of management was male. What the male manager could do, what *he* needed and how *his* future would be affected. This Report also influenced the development of management as a specialism in its own right, for which intensive education and training are necessary. By the early 1970s, management courses were acknowledged by the industrial, commercial and academic worlds as an integral part of essential training for managers and potential managers.

Equally by the early 1970s, women's questions were well to the fore. The 1970s were a time of unprecedented interest in women's opportunities, expressed in two major Acts of Parliament* and supported by widespread changes in social attitudes; by the influx of women (particularly married women) on to the labour market; and by a rising tide of women with high qualifications and aspirations. In the management field, this was characterized by, for example;

The marked increase in the numbers of women enrolling on University management courses (from 187 in 1973 to 770 in 1977);

As a proportion of all management students, the percentage rose from 12–27 per cent;

From early 1970s, there was a 33 per cent increase in women graduates entering industrial employment;

Number of women in finance and accounting rose from 14–23 per cent, and in marketing, selling and buying from 28–36 per cent.

In short then, there were several trends during the 1970s which seemed to point to a very optimistic future for women in management;

Steady moves towards a uniform commitment at the top of most major organizations to the principle of equal opportunities for women;

Increase in the numbers of women undertaking management training;

Increase in the numbers of women entering professional/management grades from which, *in theory*, it could be predicted that some at least would reach the top.

* Equal Pay Act 1970 and Sex Discrimination Act 1975

Yet now, in the early 1980s, *the fact* is that women at the top are still noticeable by their scarcity: the 1982 New Earnings Survey shows that women were just below 1 in 40 of top earners (which is a very marginal improvement on the 1968 figures showing that women were just over 1 in 50 of the top earners), and in managerial positions as a whole, women are still a small minority with only approximately 9 per cent of managers being women.

So what has happened to all those women who set out on the right road during the last decade?

What has prevented them from making their way up the organizational ladder to the upper, middle and senior management positions?

Is it too early for this influx to be showing itself at higher levels, or have we still left too many barriers *en route*?

Clearly progress to date has been disappointing. And a time of economic recession would not appear to be the best time for promoting equal opportunities.

But there are conflicting trends:

On the negative side Women's jobs are endangered and women, particularly part-time women, are in danger of being selected first for redundancy. There has been a decline in the total number of women workers and a substantial number of women have disappeared from the work scene altogether. It is likely that still more women will be lost in official statistics in the future as the new method of calculating unemployment figures, based on those applying for unemployment benefit, ignores more and more women who do not qualify for this payment.

On the positive side There is an increasing awareness of the need to introduce positive action programmes into personnel policies. Instances can be found in the Civil Service Report of the Review Committee on Women's Equality in the Civil Service and in the Treasury's own positive action programme. It can be found in similar programmes being considered, for example, by a number of leading companies in the financial and industrial world as well as in local government. Additionally, there has been an increase in the number of designations for positive training for one sex only under Section 47 of the Sex Discrimination Act. From a very slow start up to 1979 when the number of designations was only one, we now have 30 organizations designated and several applications still in the pipeline.

This reflects a recognition by senior management that at a time of economic pressure we need to maximize and utilize all resources: including female labour power. If management is investing in the training of human resources then it is necessary to get the maximum return from that investment. One way of doing this is to ensure by positive action that the education and training of women is used to the maximum.

Furthermore, and again, because of the economic recession, work patterns are becoming more flexible and the more flexible the work patterns are, the easier it is for women with their responsibilities to accommodate a dual role. By the same token however, men are going to have more time to undertake their share of responsibility in the home; the distinction between principal and secondary wage earner is becoming more blurred and the way is open for greater sharing in all directions between the husband and wife. In other words, sharing the dual role.

These changes of themselves are not going to ensure equality. They must deliberately be used as a means of equalizing the opportunities and the responsibilities between men and women. They must also be accompanied by changes in personnel practices and procedures within companies, positively designed to ensure that women are not overlooked either in formal or in informal networks leading to greater experience and opportunities for advancement. For these reasons the EOC placed great value upon the joint EOC/UMIST conference which was the basis for this book.

Baroness Lockwood
Immediate Past Chairman
Equal Opportunities Commission

Preface

By the start of the 1980s, over 42 per cent of the total workforce in the U.K. were women, with 62 per cent of all women between the ages of 16 and 60 working either part-time or full-time, the highest proportion of working women of any country in the E.E.C. Over 60 per cent of these women worked in three service industries: clerical and related; education, health and welfare; and catering, cleaning and other personal services; with clerical workers by far the biggest grouping. Women are not only concentrated in the low-status industries, but at the bottom levels of these industries. For example, whereas women represent just under 75 per cent of all clerical and related workers, they account for only 19 per cent of office managers. Indeed, a recent report of the U.K. government's Manpower Services Commission shows that in the U.K. only 20 per cent of all managers are women and if we exclude those women managers who work in clerical offices, wholesale/retail concerns and in hotels and catering, the figure drops to 10 per cent, with only 8 per cent in general management posts. Although this situation exists to some extent in other countries in Western Europe, the plight of women managers in the U.K. is one of the worst in the E.E.C.

The position of women in management is particularly important because of two distinct trends in Europe, which can be illustrated by reference to the U.K. First, the U.K. government's Manpower Services Commission forecasts that of the 200,000 jobs that are estimated to be created between 1983 and 1985, 140,000 will go to women because they are in industries which are dominated by women. At the same time, the Warwick University's Manpower Research Group estimates a decline of 850,000 in men's employment, with only a small drop in women's employment in the U.K. Second, more and more women are entering the field of management, not only because the traditional female occupations of teaching, social work and other public-sector jobs are being severely cut back in most low (if not zero) growth Western economies, but also because women feel they can attain success in management.

The U.K. University Statistical Record shows, from the early to late 1970s, that there was a 33 per cent increase in women graduates entering industrial employment: the number of women in finance and accounting rose from 14 per cent to 23 per cent in that period; in legal work from 25 per cent to 32 per cent; in personnel management from 51 per cent to 62 per cent; and in marketing, selling and buying from 28 per cent to 36 per cent. This trend has been reinforced by the increasing number of women taking university courses in management. Examining the three largest university undergraduate courses in management in the U.K., the number of female management students rose from 187 in 1973 to 770 in 1977 and is estimated at nearly 1,000 now. As a proportion of the total management students in the U.K., women management students increased from roughly 10 per cent in 1973 to well over 40 per cent in 1980; and it is estimated that they will represent nearly 50 per cent of the graduates from management and business schools in only three year's time. Similar upward trends are occurring in the United States with the percentage of women enrolled in graduate business schools in 1979 being 17 per cent at Chicago University's School of Business Administration; 25 per cent at Harvard Business School; 26 per cent at Stanford Business School; and 35 per cent at Columbia University.

With the increase of women in management, organizations are having to develop more positive action programmes to enhance career opportunities. This book will highlight some of the major issues and problems of women managers and what can be done to help them.

It is based on a conference sponsored by the Equal Opportunities Commission and attended by six major U.K. companies. The issues discussed and the strategies for positive action will be emphasized in this volume. The book explores the problems of women in management, the difficulties at each level of the managerial hierarchy, the choices open to women managers, the attitudes of male managers towards women at work and management training for women. The second section of the book will highlight the problems experienced by women in different industries and contexts; in television and radio, and in marketing and service industries. These are areas where women have been working for some time and as you will see, very little has been done to encourage and develop their management role.

The authors of these chapters are women at the front line who know the problems and make some reasonable suggestions about how one can begin to develop women managers in these contexts. The third section will concentrate on developing positive action programmes, how we can prepare a positive action programme in an organization, the experiences of an Equal Opportunities Manager in a large organization and the corporate policies for developing women managers in the U.S.A.

Cary L. Cooper
Marilyn J. Davidson

List of contributors

Elizabeth Ball
Positive Action Project Officer
National Council for Civil Liberties

William R. Brough
Equal Opportunity Programmes Manager
IBM United Kingdom Ltd

Sue Greenfeld
Associate Professor of Management
(Former Chairperson of Womens Interest Group of the American
Academy of Management)
Women's Programme in Management
University of Baltimore, USA

Olwyn Hocking
Senior Production Journalist
BBC

Sandra Langrish–Clyne
Lecturer
Department of Adult & Higher Education
University of Manchester

Sheila Rothwell
Director
The Centre for Employment Policy Studies
The Management College, Henley

Mike Smith
Senior Lecturer in Occupational Psychology
Department of Management Sciences
UMIST

Hester Thomas
Marketing Officer
ICI Paints Division

Susan Rawson Zacur
Associate Professor
Women's Programme in Management
University of Baltimore, USA

Section 1 Issues in Developing Women Managers

1 Positive action on women's career development: an overview of the issues for individuals and organizations
Sheila Rothwell

INTRODUCTION

Change – technological, organizational or individual – is the major theme of most management meetings and publications today. While the implications are wide, the process has to be managed in segments: for personnel people this usually means a fresh look at corporate training and development strategies. This is, I believe, our starting point for this subject. How does an organization ensure the appropriate development of its men and women? – and by 'appropriate', I mean matching the needs of both the business and the individuals (Stewart, 1982). This may mean, on the one hand, enabling the individuals to acquire skills that the organization needs, and on the other hand, structuring the opportunities available within the organization in such a way that the individuals can contribute more effectively.

This involves positive action in the form of organization development, management development, manager development, and manager training processes (Temporal, 1982). Yet once it becomes clear that we are focussing primarily on managerial employees, if we are talking in terms of 'development' and 'career', it also tends to be assumed that we are talking about men, since management still seems to be seen as a masculine role. Then the next question to be asked, if we are genuinely concerned with *appropriate* development and change, is: when or in what ways may it be appropriate to treat individual men and women managers differently or to treat them similarly. All too often, one suspects, they are treated similarly, when they should be treated differently, and differently when they should be treated in the same way. Almost all 'career development' is a form of positive action – for certain groups or individuals. But, if we ask which groups and individuals, the answer hitherto has been largely managers and largely men, whether in intention or in effect.

ANALYSIS OF NEED AND SUPPLY

Any re-appraisal of corporate development strategies has to start with an analysis of the needs of the business – what state is it in, what are the major plans for the 1980s?

New markets, products, services?
Changes in location, structures, unit size?
New techniques, work flows, information flows?
New accountabilities, cost consciousness, productivity measures?

How will these needs be translated into 'people' terms, and in particular, what types of organization structures, career paths and managerial skills are likely to be needed? Some sort of consensus seems to emerge that sought-after qualities include:

Flexibility,
Cost consciousness,
Inter-personal skills,
Responsiveness to external environment,
Ability to cope with pressure,
Initiative.

Whether these skills are likely to be found in one person, and indeed, whether they are really appropriate to the particular phase of that organization's life cycle or that function's stage of development (*Business Week*, 1980) are questions that are not always asked. For example, entrepreneurial skills may be appropriate at a new stage or a crisis stage of an organization; professional skills (engineering, systems analysis, marketing) may be those most needed by expanding businesses or functions; while administrative skills may be more valuable to a more settled function or 'mature' company, or in a public-sector bureaucracy. It is in the 'role culture' organization that formal management development systems are most usually found; in a 'task' culture they are more open-ended; while in 'power' culture development promotion opportunities are more personalized and subjective (Handy, 1976).

Logically, any analysis of 'business' need and 'people' need then has to be followed by an analysis of the existing 'supply', actual or potential, of managerial (and other) skills (Smith, E, 1982). Then, if there appears to be a mismatch, the next question to be asked is 'do we need more, fewer, or different people?'

At the present time, many organizations find themselves in the midst of contradictions:

The need for greater integration and centralization, but the trend towards smaller units, separate profit centres;

The need to cut labour costs and employ fewer people *but* the need for more managerial and more specialist skills;

Traditional assumptions that organizations are able to select and develop the managers they need for the next twenty years, but a climate of very rapid change and new attitudes to family and career roles.

Yet, many organizations are also beginning to realize what the most successful companies have long demonstrated: that a 'people' development emphasis is an essential ingredient of business success. It is not just a luxury in the good times; but has to be worked at even harder in the downturns. And many managers are also realizing that, however painful, 'getting rid of people' is easy: developing and making more productive those that remain is the real challenge. To meet this properly may demand real innovation: at the very least it is likely to demand some fresh thinking about career development and some changed activities. Different dimensions of analysis are needed and the development or training implications of the business plans have to be looked at in relation to different grades, divisions and occupations. The 'sex' dimension should be one of these and yet is often more likely to be ignored than 'age' as a relevant factor. Certainly, any analysis of women's career development has to start off with this sort of audit, and provides at the very least a basis for comparison with men's career development.

While it is necessary to know the numbers and percentages of women in different managerial grades (e.g. out of total numbers employed, in supervisory and lower management, in middle management, in senior management), this can only give the broad picture: more detailed analysis by department, function or earnings is likely to be equally important in understanding the situation.

Computerized personnel information systems can facilitate this analysis and enable trends to be monitored, while manpower modelling systems can enable possible change strategies to be explored. Again, it must be emphasized that this sort of analysis should not remain in isolation – it has to be fitted back into the 'Rubik Cube' of the organization's development needs, once significant patterns or key blockage points are identified and some of the reasons for them explored.

Comparison with the national picture may give some guidance as to how 'typical' your organization is, in occupational terms, but does not take you very far. Research at Ashridge has demonstrated how 'blockages' to women's career development were found at similar grade/salary levels across a variety of organizations and

Table 1.1 Women managers as a percentage of all managers in selected occupational groups U.K., 1979

Managerial group	% Managers who are women
General Management	Not available
Managerial	
Production, works and maintenance	20.3
Managers and works foremen	4.6
Site and other managers (building and civil engineering)	2.9
Transport managers	3.4
Managers in warehousing and materials handling	2.7
Office managers	19.1
Managers in wholesale and retail distribution	30.4
Publicans, restauranteurs and club stewards	41.6
All managers, but excluding those in office, wholesale and retail distribution, publicans, restauranteurs and club stewards	10.1

Source: EEC Labour Force Survey 1979

industries and aids to managers for developing detailed diagnostic procedures have been published (Ashridge, 1980; Manpower Services Commission, 1981).

REASONS FOR LACK OF DEVELOPMENT

On the assumption that analysis is likely to show that women's careers tend to stop at a disproportionately low level in the organization and that this should be seen as a 'problem', since it represents the under-utilization of a valuable organizational resource – the next question needs to be 'so what can be done about it?' Further analysis of the reasons will first be necessary, however, since the relative significance of these will vary – and without this sort of questioning, appropriate solutions are unlikely to be identified.

On the basis of 'problem-solving' techniques (Jackson, 1975), if a *problem* can be defined as *objective* plus *obstacle*, and if the objective is 'more effective development of the organization's human (including female) resources', what are the obstacles to be overcome? Research (Ashridge, 1980) has shown that the reasons for under-development of women's careers tend to fall into roughly three equal categories:

Career paths/personnel procedures,
Women's attitudes and behaviour,
Organization climate.

Career Paths/Personnel Procedures

Management development is largely a function of the career paths and personnel procedures, both formal and informal, of an organization. These constitute a series of gates and hurdles, or obstacles, by which individual career progress is facilitated, diverted or blocked. They are rarely overtly discriminatory.

Most large companies audited their processes seven or eight years ago to check there was no legal contravention. Yet there is rarely any regular monitoring of practices to see (a) how far traditional patterns of *behaviour* still persist on the part of managers or other employees, or (b) what are the *effects* of seemingly legitimate, normal personnel policies on women's and on men's career development. Which careers are blocked and which developed?

(a) *Recruitment*
Very many jobs are still seen as 'men's' or 'women's' jobs and research has shown that these patterns of job segregation, both horizontal and vertical, have not changed significantly in the 1980s (Hakim, 1981). Moreover, young women are more likely to be taken on for jobs (often requiring only 'O' level or CSE qualifications) while young men are appointed to career positions demanding 'A' level or graduate qualifications. Sometimes this is justified on the grounds of the young men's 'scientific' qualifications, despite the fact that little or no use is ever made of these qualifications in very many instances. If initial intakes to the organization for particular career routes are unbalanced, it is, of course, unlikely that the pattern will improve later, particularly in organizations with strong internal labour markets and a policy of 'promotion from within' where possible. Reliance on very limited sources of candidates, on traditional wording and placing of advertisements, on recruitment literature illustrating men managers, or on job specifications worded in terms of 'he and 'his', may be just as influential as the short-listing, interviewing and selection process, in filtering out potential women.

Yet these processes themselves are still highly inadequate in many instances and organizations finding that they are failing to recruit effective managers (of either sex) may be looking at these afresh (Hesmondhalgh, 1980). Research shows, however, that many interviewers still assume that the managerial qualities they are seeking are more likely to be found in a man than a woman, and 'relevant experience' is defined largely in terms of the experience which men will have rather than women (Hunt, 1975, 1981).

Nor is a blanket refusal to appoint a woman (blacks, Jews, . . .) to a top-level position completely a thing of the past, according to anecdotal evidence of high-flier women candidates and 'headhunter' recruitment consultants.

(b) *Training and Development*
Initial training of graduate recruits may be very much the same for young men and women across the organization, so that all start from a common base. But after that it is likely to become much more specialized and discretionary, depending on the department. The

trend now seems to be to keep graduate trainees in a specialist area for the first 2–5 years, in order to give them real responsibility, rather than moving them every few months to give them a 'taste' of a range of functions at first. This puts much more onus on the initial placement: if a woman graduate is put into a specialist personnel, programmer analyst, or research post, she is likely only to get training relative to that specialism and later to be regarded as too narrow for a broader management appointment.

Yet the need for broader 'generalist' rather than narrow specialist managers is an increasingly voiced requirement for managers in the 1980s. (Routledge and Elliot, 1982; Savage, 1981). This is usually acquired through a complementary mix of cross-functional experience and training courses. Able women are frequently kept in one specialist area – often personnel, training or planning – rather than given wider experience, as bright young men would be. This has been noted at Henley – The Management College when interviewing applicants for its Women's Scholarship Scheme on the General Management Course, finding in many instances that women's experience has simply been too limited for them to benefit sufficiently or for them to contribute to such a course.

How are people selected for courses, or vice-versa? It may be that women get on some internal courses, but few external. An Ashridge survey found that 90 per cent of women were there because they had personally requested it. Henley has had only one woman manager nominated to its General Management Course by a private-sector organization in the past five years.

Formal training courses may not be the only, or even the main development method – there may (especially in the current climate) be greater emphasis on self-development (Mumford, 1980) or on 'coaching' – but this still puts an onus on the personnel manager or the boss, to talk this through, so that it genuinely takes place and is appropriate.

Another major developmental experience for young managers may be work in special project teams or seconded short-term assignments, which give them greater visibility and contacts, and widen their experience and expertise. Women may lose out inadvertently in this process.

(c) *Appraisal System*
Training and promotion tend to be closely linked to a formal

appraisal process in most organizations. Many are very aware of the shortcomings of their system and the need for more training of their managers in operating it – but there is little discussion (or monitoring) of sex-role issues (Walker, 1983; Stewart and Stewart, 1977). Do some (or most) men find it even more difficult to appraise women honestly than they do men – is there a greater tendency to avoid discussion of weaknesses and give an impression that everything is very satisfactory, or even very good, but then to rate them as 'not fitted for promotion', as one Civil Service analysis showed (Corby, 1983). It may be easy for factors such as 'passivity' or 'lack of initiative' to be accepted as unchangeable on the one hand, because they fit the manager's stereotype of a woman; while on the other hand another woman may be marked down as 'too aggressive' for behaviour that would have been rated positively in a young man. Coaching is needed if her 'passivity' or 'aggression' is really an obstacle to her becoming an effective manager.

On the other hand, if appraisal schemes really concentrated on performance and achievement, measured as objectively as possible, women might be rated more highly, as they often seem to put much more effort into doing a good job than into being seen to do it, so they miss the recognition they deserve.

(d) *Promotion*
Even with internal advertising and formalized interviewing, this still tends to be a highly subjective process, which needs continual monitoring to ensure it is non-discriminatory in effect. Without it, reliance on word-of-mouth and personal nomination by senior men managers maximizes the subjective nature of the process, which the interview system is then likely to re-inforce (Savage, 1982).

There also tend to be certain patterns or 'tracks' of appointments which traditionally lead to the top or are taken by high-fliers. If these include posts which no woman has ever held, how equal is the opportunity in practice?

A 'geographical mobility' requirement may be a barrier in some cases. Although many organizations are already modifying these requirements, because of men's changing attitudes, some are tightening them up in the changed situation of economic recession. Women may be deliberately discouraged from seeking promotion by exaggerating potential travelling or moving house requirements, which are likely to be infrequent or flexible in practice.

A fourth major obstacle to promotion is always the fact that a woman is likely to have a baby and leave. Yet it is a vicious circle: if they are not promoted, then they may well leave – for a more creative alternative. The timing of both the decision to leave and whether or not to return may be affected by management policy, but this is often ignored as an area of management responsibility.

(e) *Family Policies*
The extent to which an organization's formal policies make provision for maternity leave adjustments, flexible working time (hours per day, days per week, or weeks per year) or re-entry facilities, is likely to affect most critically of all the extent to which it is able to keep its women and realize its 'investment' in them. If there are no such policies, then even a discussion of career and family plans is unlikely to take place. Some American research has indicated that women's career decisions are more likely to determine family decisions than vice versa (Hoffman, 1980).

Lack of child-care facilities and the decline of many state and employer-sponsored day-care schemes in recent years has been well documented (Equal Opportunities Commission, 1978). Yet combined employer/local authority facilities or the provision of assisted places on privately run schemes may still be an option worth considering as a means of retaining valuable staff (McCroskey, 1982). Another alternative is the provision of child-care assistance as an optional 'benefit' or 'perk' as an alternative to a company car or suit-hire, similar to assisted school fees.

(f) *Pay and Benefits*
Despite the Equal Pay Act, it is not necessarily correct to assume that a young woman will be getting the same salary as a young man –at least after three years in the organization. In large organizations with formal salary structures, inequalities may be less likely to creep back in unnoticed, but the scope for rewarding rises on merit, promotion, or other grounds, varies considerably. Job evaluation schemes are not necessarily free from sex bias, or subjective assumptions about the value of work done by women (Lupton and Bowey, 1983; Equal Opportunities Commission, 1981a).

Other discretionary benefits may still show considerable discrepancies – pensions, low-interest mortgage schemes, and company cars in particular, are benefits on which women managers lose out in comparison to men.

Women's Attitudes and Behaviour

(a) Lack of Confidence

Women's lack of confidence in themselves is found time and time again in research studies as the biggest inhibiting factor in women's career development – and the main reason why most of us will go along (to some extent) with the statement that 'women are their own worst enemies'. The origins of this in women's upbringing and socialization, and even some of the remedies for it, are not hard to find, but what is most important is the *recognition* of it, by themselves and their managers.

Then the manifestations of it – low career orientation, apparent lack of leadership and initiative, inability to build on success, unwillingness to accept promotion – and all the seeming shortcomings of women and why they are not 'seen' as managers become more explicable.

At the same time it is important not to go too far down the 'blame the victim' path – since these responses are rational in a situation in which opportunities are (or were, until recently in most firms) very limited. Similar reactions may be found by unsuccessful men, or by other minority groups as Kanter's analysis of 'the moving' and the 'stuck' has demonstrated (Kanter, 1977).

She has shown that looking at an organization in terms of its opportunity structure, the power capacity of certain positions in it, and its social composition often reveals marked distinctions between 'high' and 'low' opportunity positions, which in turn, breed two very different types of involvement in work and thus two different types of people (whether individuals or groups): the 'moving' and 'the stuck'. Much of the behaviour that has been attributed to women in the work place emerges as behaviour characteristic of 'stuckness', for men who are stuck exhibit the same tendencies.

(b) Competitiveness

Women's personal beliefs in their own abilities may be high at the same time as they find it difficult to be competitive with men about it – they tend to believe that, by working hard and 'doing a good job' (often 120 per cent of what is necessary) they will be noticed and promoted. Whereas, in practice, they tend to be left to continue

Table 1.2 Characteristics of people's involvement in work

Moving	Stuck
Behave in ways that confirm their selection for advancement	Behave in ways that confirm organization's lack of attention to them
High and rising aspirations	Limited and lowering aspirations
Motivated to achieve	Appear less motivated
High self-esteem	Under-rate and under-value their abilities
See and use more skills	Perceive themselves as inadequately skilled
Volunteer for new challenges	Reluctant to opt for assignments beyond their previous experience
Highly work-engaged	Major life involvements and satisfactions sought outside work.
Highly committed to organization	Dream of escape elsewhere (own business/family)
Prepare themselves for the next job	Perfect details and acceptance of present job
Express dissatisfactions actively and constructively	Gripe passively about personal details; conservative resistance

Source: Adapted from Kanter, 1977

that job – while the man who puts more effort into getting on well with the boss and to preparing himself for the next job will be the one who gets it. This is, of course, partly a question of '*politics*' and of the masculine organizational game. If women are less skilled at this or feel a strong distaste for this sort of competitiveness, they may lose out, despite high ability and motivation. And recent attitude surveys of men and women managers in the U.S.A. have tended to show very little difference between them on very many indicators of experience and potential, other than in certain types of power, where more men seek and obtain power, over information and over budgets. (Harlan and Weiss, 1981)

(c) *Family Roles*
Women's family roles – as daughters, wives or mothers – re-inforce not only 'dependent' attitudes and the ease with which they can

assimilate organizational rejection and turn to domestic fulfilment instead, but also create very real stresses and pressures, both psychological and physical.

Psychological stress is created by the need to conform to socially induced images of femininity and to be the perfect wife, mother and homemaker. This produces many conflicts and burdens of guilt which inhibit career ambition and performance. Physical stress and exhaustion from fulfilling two demanding roles often exacerbates this – whether women are single, married, with or without children (Cooper and Davidson, 1982). Many women still feel the need to choose between children and career in a way that men do not, even if they can (just about) cope with the strains of marriage.

If management is typically seen as a male role, this is still the most difficult aspect for women to cope with, since they are still primarily stereotyped into an, at least partial, family/domestic role, even if their interest in that aspect of their life is considerably less than that of many men managers. Greenhalgh has shown that career patterns of single women are still more akin to those of other women, than of single or married men (Greenhalgh, 1980). Those who are seeking, covertly or overtly, to achieve an appropriate balance of responsibilities are criticized for 'wanting it both ways', and 'lacking commitment'.

(d) *Stereotyping*

Those women managers who do 'make it to the top' by virtue of their isolation and their conformity to masculine career requirements, have in the past often been single and have often been seen as 'neurotics' by other women (as well as by men). Thus, they have neither served as 'role models' for younger women, nor helped them to climb the ladder in turn.

Thus, because women are unused to seeing themselves as managers, have rarely worked for one, and may also hold negative stereotypes of them, petty conflicts and jealousies are often said to arise between women who have previously worked well together when one or the other is promoted. They find this difficult to handle and it may provide a further reason for reluctance to accept promotion and lose peer support. Such problems are not, of course, unknown among men, but are less likely to be used as an excuse by higher-level men for not offering promotion, or deter most men from accepting it.

The four patterns briefly discussed above also illustrate *stereotypes* of women's attitudes and behaviour which tend to hold back their advancement as much as their actual attitudes and behaviour because the implications drawn from them reinforce the underlying beliefs of many men managers that 'women managers' is really a contradiction in terms (Hennig and Jardim, 1979). By virtue of their visibility and isolation, women are either seen as too 'feminine', thus not really 'managers', or 'non-conformist' and thus not really 'women' or 'not our sort'. Frequently found feminine roles with which women are labelled tend to be: the 'pet' who passively goes along with things and is the recipient of compliments rather than power (see (a) above); the 'mistress' who uses her femininity to achieve success, but is either not taken seriously because of it, or arouses counter-productive resentments (see (a) and sometimes (b) above); the 'mother' who looks after everyone and makes them feel good, without seeking advancement herself, since her 'domestic' role is important (see (c) above); the non-conformists are the 'women's-libber' who reveals male chauvinism (see (b) above) or the 'iron-maiden', who is a forceful achiever, but at a cost (d). These stereotypes are probably most strongly held at the highest level of the organization where, even in industries employing a lot of women, or in the public sector, few senior women are found.

Organization Climate

The ethos of an organization and especially the style and personalities of its top managers is likely to have a major impact on the scope and pattern of career development there. It may affect the women's opportunities – both independently and in conjunction with the other two factors – since a very positive attitude can, in itself, ensure the career development of some women, regardless of the other factors and a very negative attitude will mean that no women advance beyond a certain low level, except in an occasional specialist sideline, 'suitable' for a woman.

What is most frequently found, however, is lip-service support for women's career development on the part of senior management, coupled with indifference to doing anything about it, particularly anything that seems to be treating women differently from men, since this could be rationalized as discrimination.

Nevertheless, where the organization climate is orientated towards people development and in general seeks to establish participatory attitudes, open relationships and readiness to change, there is greater scope for women's career development, if reinforced by the personnel policies and women's own attitudes. Unfortunately, under the exigencies of recession, some organizations are tending to become more narrow, autocratic and formalized as they concentrate on the cost-cutting necessary for survival. The pressures of contraction are tending to shorten management hierarchies and reduce opportunities for promotion at the same time as a renewed emphasis on cost-effectiveness makes it all too easy for any suggestion of action to develop women's careers to seem a non-essential luxury.

STRATEGIES FOR CHANGE

The search for appropriate strategies for organizational change, especially change involving the adoption of new technologies in many aspects of the business, and for strategies of management development appropriate to that, are currently a major preoccupation of many organizations, consultants and writers. As Taylor commented 'in practice, Strategic Planning, Staff Development and Organisation Development are most effective when they are conceived and implemented as a combined operation' (Taylor, 1983; Tichy, 1982). Women's career development, therefore, needs to be strategically planned within such a broad overall strategy.

Initial diagnosis of the situation and identification of the gaps and blockages should highlight some of the priority needs – but important decisions have to be made as to whether to concentrate on moving up women from areas where there are already a lot employed – such as offices – or to try to get them into areas where there are at present very few, such as factory or technical management, and where, because of current shortages or real innovation, there are fresh opportunities. Using 'force-field' analysis, one would probably decide to build on strengths – yet an area of shortage, innovation or crisis may provide a better opportunity to start in some situations, particularly at a time of major upheaval and re-organization, where radical innovation is needed. Much therefore depends on the other priorities of the organization at the time and attempts to develop women's careers must work through and with those, not in isolation (unless it is felt that, while the major focus of attention is elsewhere, a 'pilot' developmental scheme could be slipped in unnoticed!). The 'politics' of change and innovation apply no less (and probably more) to the issue of equal opportunity positive action than to any other.

The strategies and tactics available to help achieve organization change in general – and career development in particular – are well known to most personnel managers (Margerison, 1978; Kotter and Scheslinger, 1979). Success is only likely to come from getting the mix that is appropriate for the individual and the organization. They can be broadly grouped into 'structural and procedural' approaches, 'personal and individual', and 'attitudinal'. These three categories broadly correspond to the 'obstacle' areas identified above and discussion of them may have already suggested possibilities for change. They include 'developmental' and 'structural' tactics (Burgoyne, 1983; Lyons, 1982).

Changing Structures and Procedures

(a) Managerial Appointments

Continual scrutiny of recruitment and promotion procedures is still necessary to eliminate unconscious sex bias at all stages. Positive literature – like the booklet produced by GEC Research, can illustrate determination to encourage the development of women in science and engineering. But target numbers or percentages do need to be set and monitored. This may appear to smack of quota-setting and abhorrence is usually expressed at the idea of importing such 'dangerous' American practices. While they are, in any case, unlawful here, in that appointments have to be made on a non-discretionary basis, it *is* lawful to make a particular effort to encourage more women (or men) to apply or to develop them for it, if there have been no (or very few) women (or men) in that position or occupation previously (Sex Discrimination Act, s.48). Moreover, very many individual and organization goals are normally set in terms of a percentage increase/decrease target, in terms of output, scrap, sales, etc., and some companies apply it to almost all forms of objective setting where there is serious intent to achieve results. The same could be done to increase the number of women in management: nor is there any need for this to mean 'tokenism' or appointment of less able managers. It could provide just the 'new blood' and 'fresh outlook' that many organizations realize they need in their managers at the present time.

If interviewing is still the main selection tool – training for it (if any) needs to take full account of those bias problems, and the results need to be monitored. The use of selection tests and assessment centre techniques can also have pitfalls, but may serve as additional, more *objective* indicators, of both potential and performance in the real skills required. Some interesting developments of these techniques have been made by South-West Gas and by IBM, for example.

Analysis of the qualities needed for managerial work in the eighties is likely to put higher emphasis on inter-personal skills and group working, where women are often thought to be better. But this is itself something of a stereotyped judgement, and it is likely that the range of abilities exists among women as it does among men – creative and entrepreneurial skills are just as likely to be found among women, given the numbers rising in the media and advertising world, for example. The challenge to management lies in a more open-minded approach to selection and evaluation of 'relevant experience', in matching the required skills to the organizational needs at a particular time. Nor should women's experiences outside the labour market be ignored when considering their abilities – running voluntary work activities and finances, or organising family activities and domestic budgets, often calls for qualities of flexibility, resilience and planning beyond those required of many men in routine management positions.

(b) *Organization Structures*

If organizations are restructuring into smaller units and profit centres or making more use of project teams (or quality circles, at lower levels), then new opportunities are opened up for women to take responsibility. These changes probably necessitate new succession plans and planned 'experience' moves. If women have hitherto been invisible or ignored in traditional procedures, advantage can be taken of the new situation to develop them as well.

Moreover, the shortenings of hierarchies and reduction of promotion opportunities are necessitating more *horizontal* moves in many organizations – these can facilitate the widening of women's experience, to overcome any handicap of narrow specialist expertise. 'Temporary secondment' can also facilitate this.

'Bridging' occupations often need to be created to provide a move out of a traditional 'dead end' position – such as office supervisor or 'personal assistant', to get women moving up the management ladder at all. But the introduction of new technology is often creating these sorts of requirements in any case. For example, developments in office technology may necessitate close liaison with management services and acquisition of an understanding of computer technology. This may, in turn, facilitate a move into those departments or out of them into a marketing function. As information technology integrates departments in new ways, so new occupations are needed and, while there is no need for them to become male-dominated, they will be unless positive efforts are made – despite the fact that it is women who often have the 'hands-on' experience and expertise, and only need assistance in being seen as and in seeing themselves as 'technically capable'.

(c) *Appraisal Systems*
Unless managers are themselves appraised on how well they develop their subordinates – including women – they are unlikely to consider it important. How this can come to be built into the system will depend on how it is operated, and modified or what training is given in any particular organization. Advice given by the First Division Association (the Senior Civil Servants' Trade Union) asks managers reporting on subordinates, or serving on promotion panels, to guard against taking a negative view of a woman's capabilities or prospects, based largely on her known, or likely, family responsibilities, rather than the quality of her work. The report stated:

'In addition a study of ATs found that whereas there is little or no relationship between entrants sex and their FSB marks, men were subsequently judged to have the better long-term potential. While outstanding women are recognised, there may be a tendency to put most borderline women on the lower side of the border but to put borderline men on the upper side. Although these decisions may be unconscious they mean women receive less favourable treatment than men.

'When writing annual reports would you ever make stereotyped judgements; for example do you tend to give women higher markings for "relations with others" and lower markings for "drive and determination" or "reliability under pressure"?

'When assessing "long term potential" would you ever give a lower marking to a young female civil servant because you considered her likely to start a family and therefore give up work or at least serious career aspirations?

'Alternatively, would you perceive future potential in terms of personal characteristics and behaviour patterns which you assume are more common in one sex than another?

'The long term potential marking on the staff report is the only item not disclosed to the person appraised and so cannot easily be challenged.

'We ask you when reporting on female civil servants to avoid decisions based on stereotyped assumptions.

'We also ask you when assessing long term potential to make your decisions solely on the civil servant's capabilities and to disregard the possibility that a woman might leave the Service in future years just as you would disregard that possibility when assessing a man' (*Source:* First Division Association, 1983).'

If new methods – of peer, group, or self-appraisal – or simply of more 'open' appraisal are currently being considered (Walker, 1983), then opportunities arise for building in attention to women's career needs; such as confidence-building, financial skills, future career planning, to take account of a likely family break, or possible geographical relocation. In evaluating past performance, the current emphasis of 'good practice' is an objective evaluation of achievement, rather than subjective rating of character traits: encouragement of this could help eliminate unconscious subjective bias against women (Williams, 1981).

(d) *Working Hours*

At a time of high unemployment, reductions or changing patterns of working time are currently under discussion in most industries. Flexibility in working hours is probably the single biggest need of working women and the opportunity is now available for *serious* thought to be given to ways and means of job-sharing and/or part-time working from home, even in *managerial* work (Equal Opportunities Commission, 1981a; Goodhart, 1982). Most companies can identify posts which are made up into full-time ones as new responsibilities are added, taken away or restructured, but which could have become part-time posts. Most job descriptions are in terms of 'percentage of time allocated' and very many could be split. Issues of administrative or co-ordination costs have to be set against 'productivity' benefits and the opportunities afforded by new information technology. This will give scope for more flexibility and variety in men's careers too, particularly at a middle management 'plateau', or being asked to consider early retirement, as the Rank Xerox 'Network' system has shown. Examples of women computer professionals working from home and managed similarly can also be found at ICL and F International, (a company almost entirely organized by women on that basis). One example of a 'split' management post is that of training manager at the Stock Exchange, which is shared between a man and a woman, each taking responsibility for certain grades/types of training (Syrett, 1982; Povall and Hastings, 1983).

Plans for adjustments to working time patterns, while primarily taking account of organizational needs, also need to consider staff preference: it is important to remember that female priorities may be different from those of men (who generally opt for longer holiday entitlement) and to allow scope for these differences.

The biggest barrier to changing organizational practices to enable women's potential to be utilized is the stereotyped management belief that 'part-time equals part commitment' and thus that 'part-time management is a contradiction in terms', rather than a useful flexible option for organizations and individuals at certain stages of their development (House of Lords, 1982). A re-examination of these assumptions is drastically overdue, particularly if most organizations still plan on the assumption of a 'continuous' management career, despite contractions.

(e) *Re-entry Policies*

If a 'continuous' career is therefore a pre-requisite, other adjustments can help manage a 'family break', if this is on a 'full-time' basis, for a few years rather than a few months. More organizations seem to condemn women for leaving than to welcome them for the vacancies they will create (despite complaints about middle management 'plateaux' and 'blocked' career ladders in many organizations).

If organizations wish to realize their investment then they need to keep their women managers, and this needs effort in terms of maintaining contact, offering one-off opportunities, and managing re-entry. Specific policies, such as that at National Westminster Bank, or in the medical profession, are likely to be more effective than merely good-will and 'discretion' in individual circumstances. These involve maintaining a register of potential re-entrants, regular annual contact, and opportunities for occasional work and/ or training. The Civil Service too, has re-entry facilities, though on a less formalized basis.

The likely age of re-entry is probably 30–35, if the break is taken by women in their late twenties. Some women are, however, postponing starting a family until their thirties, when their careers are more firmly established: organizational practices as well as personal and family circumstances influence this decision, so it should also be a matter for management discussion and counselling, so that planning on both sides is more realistic. Nor is there any reason why re-entry policies should conflict with a trend to earlier retirement: they are all aspects of a more 'flexible' organizational career. Moreover, a career stretching from 20–30 and from 35–55 is still very 'respectable', even in conventional development terms. *Succession planning* can readily be modified to take account of this: it does not mean that women have to be left out of such planning because of uncertainties. In any case, lengthening promotion patterns are tending to become the norm again in a climate of contraction, which means fewer vacancies and promotions (Bennison, 1979).

Changing Men and Women

(a) Training and Development Plans
The use of 'courses', whether internal or external, is still seen as a major technique for change in both individual and organizational terms. Not only do more women need to be sent on courses in a similar way to men, but thought also needs to be given to the appropriateness of the timing, contents and organization of these courses. For example, questions of the timing (week, day, or weekend) and location (on site, at a distance) still need discussion and consideration. It should not be assumed that women will never want to go on weekend or on residential courses, nor that they can automatically do this as readily as most men can: individual circumstances have to be taken into account and some counselling

may be needed as to ways of adjusting domestic responsibilities if the experience is novel and if there is some reluctance for these reasons.

Course methods, literature and case studies may still need revision – since most have traditionally been based on a concept of management as a masculine profession. Whether course syllabus content needs to change is doubtful – but scope for discussion of the implications for society, work and managers of changing sex roles needs to be built into all the 'behavioural' subjects and some of the others (such as marketing). Henley has been giving considerable thought to these issues, partly as a result of Women's Scholarship Scheme (on which questionnaire evaluations have been generally positive) (Rothwell, 1982).

While most courses need to include opportunities to discuss the problems of men and women working together, or be specially aimed at that (Hammond and Hastings, 1982), the use of *women-only* courses on occasions needs serious consideration. These can enable various women to overcome some of their own attitude problems (identified in the previous section), either through discussion or assertiveness training. They are not a substitute for mixed courses but women managers who have experienced them (although initially resistant to the idea, like most other women) have found them tremendously helpful (Fonda and Paul, 1982; Berman, 1982).

The question of training men to cope with these issues is only just beginning to be tackled, but experience is showing the value of role-play exercises and discussions, especially when led by men trainers and consultants (Dyar, 1982; Smith, M, 1982). Future research is likely to give more attention to the issue, since training aimed only at making women more like men is not likely to be very effective in the long run.

Since more organizations are now putting more emphasis on in-house or 'tailored' external courses, there is more scope for women's, or men's special needs to be included. A 'Distance Learning' package, such as that offered by Henley, might be especially valuable for women who are at a part-time stage of their career, or preparing for re-entry.

The other great current emphasis in management development is self-development. If women are traditionally passive about this, or unaware of the politics of organizational opportunities, they may be in particular need of advice and assistance. Similarly, men managers may need extra help in acting as 'mentors' or in 'coaching' women subordinates – particularly if they are fearful of 'sexual harassment' accusations. Men need to be given the confidence to nominate women subordinates for challenging tasks, in the same way as they nominate their young men.

'Confidence' may be developed in the work situation in many different ways. Increasingly, the successful implementation of new technology is seen to depend on the involvement of the employees concerned. Enid Mumford (Mumford, 1983) has illustrated one method of achieving this for office staff and managers. It is also highly dependent on the skills of a project manager, who is not necessarily the technical expert, but who can manage and co-ordinate both the 'systems' and 'people' side of the development effectively. Research at Henley has found only one example of a woman in such a role (a systems manager) but she was highly effective in that case (a small electronics factory).

Pushing women into chairing meetings, making presentations, or going out to clients is hardly revolutionary – only a touch of 'positive' action to help women to overcome their own reticence, and also to increase their 'visibility' and 'contacts' in the organization (Kanter, 1977).

(b) Support Groups

Encouragement of women to form their own networks of women at different levels of the hierarchy or outside the organization, e.g. Women in Shell, Women in Banking, Women in Personnel Management (Riley, 1982) is likely to be a useful way of building confidence and expertise – and complementary to their participation in other activities of their professional institute or BIM branch. Discussions with other women can help to remove feelings of powerlessness, obtain insights into organizational politics, and enable them to identify common problems faced by women managers which are not necessarily their own 'fault' or weakness, but an aspect of the situation to be dealt with.

(c) Counselling and Career Planning

In the current climate of redundancy and change, some personnel departments (e.g. ICI) are developing these services for those who leave and even for those who remain. Women who have not previously been career-minded but who develop new interests or recognize the need to stretch themselves as they mature, or as their children grow up, may be helped to develop their potential by these facilities, if they are encouraged to consult them.

(d) *Domestic Roles*
So far, my main perspective has been on organizational needs and on men and women as managers. Since part of the problem for women managers is that they are still seen outside (and even inside) work in 'a domestic' context, they need help in recognizing and reconciling these ambivalences. This is likely to include the issue of domestic chores – how can these be planned and organized as effectively as paid work (for which there has been training), or will they continue to be done in traditionally wasteful and time-consuming ways? If they are shared with a partner – is the woman wary about taking on all the essential 'day to day' things, while the man does the 'once-a-week' or 'postponable' jobs? These 'petty' issues affect time horizons and work perspectives as well.

Parenting issues and guilts need to be talked through and 'female' parents should try comparing themselves with the 'male' parents they work with, not just their own mothers (or fathers). Men need to be able to discuss the pressure of reconciling 'managerial' and 'parenting' responsibilities. They can only do this in an organizational climate that is open and supportive, rather than 'threatening' to those who admit such conflicts.

Changing Attitudes

Much that has already been said relates to changes in attitude on the part of men and women managers. It also applies to senior management and the organization climate as a whole – openness and receptivity to change is what organizational development and career development is really about. But it needs the power, resources and commitment of those at the top to make it happen; if there is a *will*, the *ways* are not difficult to find.

If there is hostility – or, more likely, indifference, which may be another way of expressing satisfaction with things the way that they are – then progress is more difficult. It is worth thinking about how senior managers' attitudes towards other issues have been changed and commitment obtained. It is highly unlikely that they will be willing to attend any sort of courses or discussion on the subject – as they might, say, on new technology. They may, however, be prepared to talk about the subject in social chit-chat, so the politics of 'keeping women on the agenda' are important: steering contact with a senior manager in a similar organization which has done something new in this area, with top-level women who might be admired, or with whom the company could do business, all needs 'arranging'.

Similarly, raising the visibility of able women already in the organization by temporary assignment to projects that give them top-level contact – or by coaching top 'token' women to help those below. But senior men need 'coaching' too – they may genuinely find it more difficult to accept a woman who is prepared to be fully mobile, for example (expecting her husband to move house to follow her, or to live separately during the week), than the woman who coyly refuses promotion involving a move, because of her husband's job.

'Efficiency' arguments tend to receive the most receptive hearing, but the costs of training always seem to be more visible – and higher – than the benefits. Nevertheless, considerable assistance is now available from MSC, EEC, and (to a lesser extent), EOC sources, to cover a proportion of any specific outlay on new courses or positive development. Women's scholarships are available on Henley's General Management and MBA Courses and at some other business schools (Rothwell, 1982). Issues of 'adult retraining' are on the national agenda for support.

Evaluation of training costs and benefits is, of course, always difficult, but some personnel directors are now making great efforts to develop criteria for this – either for their own satisfaction or to meet the needs of competitive cost-conscious colleagues. Women's development needs to be looked at in this light and the small cost of some positive action set against the very much higher costs of losing their talents, and the 'investment' already made in the hard work, ability and efficiency of existing women managers is often the subject of favourable comment by men. If this is a genuine evaluation, rather than a patronizing platitude (and most of them assure me that it is genuine) then the productivity argument should be sufficient justification for further women's management development. Getting women in on the bottom line may be the first step to getting them off the bottom rung!

CONCLUSIONS

This paper has argued that all management development is a form of positive action and that it is only necessary to take all the conventional and current aspects of the subject – such as selection, training, self-development, appraisal systems, horizontal career moves, succession planning, project assignment, organizational restructuring – and to ensure that they are implemented in such a way as to facilitate the development of women as well as of men. While some adjustments are needed, they are hardly revolutionary and do not go beyond those which could, in any case, be justified as appropriate to individuals of differing interests and abilities, or even of differing functions or sections within an organization.

As in all management development, a strategic approach is needed to ensure that a range of techniques and interventions are used and that the 'mix' of tactics and techniques is appropriate to the circumstances: a selection of both 'top-down' and 'bottom-up' approaches, and a combination of certain structural or procedural policy changes in the organization with measures to develop individuals' abilities. Similarly, careful planning is needed in scheduling these activities. The fact that they cannot all be done at once is not an argument for not attempting any of them: a five-year rolling schedule is likely to be as appropriate here as in other aspects of corporate planning, provided results are maintained and adjustments made on a similar 'rolling' basis.

But although I have argued that revolutionary change is not needed, some *change* is implied (as in all management development), and this is primarily *attitude* change (as in much other change, even technological). Even to reconceptualize thinking about management development in terms of women's careers, rather than men's, is symbolic of this implementation and demands greater effort, and it is not, in my view, likely that increased career development for women will 'just happen' left to itself, any more than it has done in the past (apart from the outstanding individuals). All change strategies need planning and a combination of the usual techniques: these have been set out (Kotter and Scheslinger, 1979) as:

Coercion,
Manipulation,
Negotiation,

Participation,
Education and communication,
Facilitation and support.

While it is likely that more of the techniques at the end of the list may be appropriate, the others should not be ignored. A measure of coercion – an act of will on the part of a senior manager – may be just as necessary to achieve initial impetus or 'unblock' a static situation as in other types of change.

A consideration of whether likely 'fast' or 'slow' implementation of change is advisable and the amount of consultation needed (and with whom) will depend on where the opposition is most likely to come from, why and how powerful it is likely to be and whose co-operation or support is essential and/or likely to be forthcoming (Kotter, 1981). This sort of analysis is often made instinctively by experienced managers planning a new course of action and it is sometimes done explicitly by a new project team. Similarly, it can usefully be applied to the planning of a management development strategy and *particularly* the issue of women's career development, since this may be perceived, covertly, at least, as threatening to men managers.

Analysis of resistance to change commonly identifies its origin in individuals' fears of losing something of value, such as money, career opportunity, job security, group cohesion, or comfortable personal relationships and in a general human inability to tolerate too much uncertainty. At a time of considerable social and organizational change such fears may be maximized, but even in relatively stable situations issues of women's career development tend to raise many of the fears mentioned above, in terms of bringing female rats into the rat race, as well as stirring deep-seated and often sub-conscious fears about sex roles and self-identity. The 'objective' dimensions of change involved may be minimal, but it is likely to be important to be aware of covert reactions and likely resistance, in order to provide the educative and supportive facilities needed, and to develop perceptions of the benefits, (Carnell, 1982) as well as of the threats, presented by such changes at various levels, but especially in the highly conservative culture of British senior management.

A time of change can be a time of opportunity: on every side there are calls for new approaches to management and for leadership and innovation in organizations: the extent to which an organization develops its women managers and effectively utilizes their creativity in its upper echelons could well be the sign and the measure of such innovation.

REFERENCES

Ashridge Management College, *Employee Potential – Issues in the Development of Women* (IPM, 1980).

Bennison, M. 'A New Approach to Career Management', *Personnel Management*, October 1979.

Berman, M 'Assertion Training', in Cooper, C. (ed.) op. cit.

Burgoyne, J. 'Management Development', in Williams, A. P. O. (ed.) op. cit.

Business Week 'Wanted: A Manager to Fit Each Strategy', 25 February 1980.

Carnell, C. *The Evaluation of Organisational Change* (Gower: Epping 1982).

Cooper, C. (ed.) *Practical Approaches to Women's Career Development* (Manpower Services Commission: Sheffield, 1982).

Cooper, C. and Davidson, M. *High Pressure: Working Lives of Women Managers* (Fontana: London, 1982).

Corby, S. 'Women in the Civil Service: Holding Back or Held Back?', *Personnel Management*, February 1983.

Dyar, D. 'Sexism in Training and Development', in Cooper, C. (ed.) op. cit.

Equal Opportunities Commission, *I Want to Work, but What About the Kids?* (E.O.C. Manchester, 1978).

Equal Opportunities Commission, *Job Evaluation Schemes Free of Sex Bias* (E.O.C. Manchester, 1981a).

Equal Opportunities Commission, *Job-Sharing* (E.O.C. Manchester, 1981b).

First Division Association, *Who Flies Highest?* (F.D.A. London, 1983).

Fonda, N. and Paul, N. 'Life/Work Planning Workshops for Women, in Cooper, C. (ed.) op. cit.

Greenhalgh, C. 'Male and Female Wage Differentials in Great Britain – is Marriage an Equal Opportunity?', *Economic Journal*, December, 1980.

Hakim, C. 'Job Segregation: Trends in the 1970s', *Employment Gazette*, December, 1981.

Hammond, V. and Hastings, C. 'Tackling Women's Issues in Courses for Men and Women', in Cooper, C. (ed.) op. cit.

Handy, C. *Understanding Organisations* (Penguin: London, 1976).

Harlan, A. and Weiss, C. *Moving Up: Women in Managerial Careers*, unpublished paper, (Wellesley College: Boston, 1981).

Hennig, M. and Jardim, A. *The Managerial Woman* (Pan: London, 1979).

Hesmondhalgh, S. 'You Know What They're Like', *Recruitment*, December, 1980.

Hoffman, L. W. 'The Employment of Women, Education and Fertility', in *Women and Achievement* Mednick, M. *et al.* (eds) (John Wiley and Sons: London, 1980).

House of Lords, *Report of Select Committee on the European Communities: Draft Directive on Voluntary Part-Time Work* (H.M.S.O.: London, 1982).

Hunt, A. *Management Attitudes and Practices Towards Women at Work* (H.M.S.O: London, 1975).

Hunt, A. 'Women and Underachievement at Work', *E.O.C. Research Bulletin*, Vol. 5, Spring 1981.

Jackson, K. F. *Art Of Solving Problems* (Heinemann: London, 1975).

Kanter, R. M. *Men and Women of the Corporation* (Basic Books: New York, 1977).

Kotter, J. P. and Scheslinger, L. A. 'Choosing Strategies for Change', *Harvard Business Review*, March–April 1979.

Lupton, T. and Bowey, A. *Wages and Salaries* (Gower: Aldershot, 2nd Edn, 1983).

Lyons, T. 'Training for New Companies', *Journal of European Industrial Training*, 6 May 1982.

Manpower Services Commission, *No Barriers Here* (M.S.C.: Sheffield, 1981).

Margerison, C. *Influencing Organisational Change* (IPM: London, 1978).

McCroskey, J. 'Work and Families, What is the Employer's Responsibility?', *Personnel Journal*, Spring 1982.

Mumford, A. *Making Experience Pay* (McGraw Hill: London 1980).

Mumford, E. *Designing Secretaries* (Manchester Business School, 1983).

Povall, M. and Hastings, J. *A Re-entry and Retainer Scheme for Women* (City University, 1983).

Povall, M. and Hastings, J. (eds), *Managing or Removing the Career Break* (Manpower Services Commission: London, 1983).

Riley, K. 'Women's Networks', in Cooper, C. (ed.) op. cit.

Rothwell, S. 'Management Courses and Women', *Ergonomics*, May 1984, Vol. 27, No. 5.

Routledge, C. W. and Elliott, C. K., 'Organisational Mobility and Career Development', *Personnel Review*, 11 March 1982.

Savage, A., 'Selecting Managers for a Permanent State of Flux', *Personnel Management*, October 1981.

Savage, A. 'Reconciling Your Appraisal System with Company Reality', *Personnel Management*, May, 1982.

Smith, E. S. 'Strategic Business Planning and Human Resources', *Personnel Journal*, August/September, 1982.

Smith, M. S. 'Avoiding the Male Backlash', in Cooper, C. (ed.) op. cit.

Stewart, A. and Stewart, V. *Practical Performance Appraisal* (Gower: Aldershot, 1977).

Stewart, R. *Choices for the Manager* (McGraw-Hill: London, 1982).

Syrett M. 'How to Make Job-Sharing Work', *Personnel Management*, October, 1982.

Taylor, B. 'Management Training and Development in the 1980s', in

Management Development and Training Handbook Taylor, B. and Lippiatt G. L. (eds), (McGraw-Hill: London, 2nd edn, 1983).

Temporal, R. P. 'Strategic Management for the 1980s', *International Journal of Management*, 3 January 1982.

Tichy, N. *et al.* 'Strategic Human Resource Management', *Sloan Management Review*, Winter 1982.

Walker, J. 'Performance Appraisal', in Williams, A. P. O. (ed.) op. cit.

Williams, A. P. O. (ed.) *Using Personnel Research* (Gower: Aldershot, 1983).

Williams, M. *Appraising Performance and Assessing Potential* (Leadership Trust: Ross-on-Wye, 1981a).

Williams, M. *Counselling and Coaching* (Leadership Trust: Ross-on-Wye, 1981b).

2 Women managers: their problems and what can be done to help them*
Marilyn J. Davidson and
Cary L. Cooper

INTRODUCTION

With more women now working than ever before, there is also an enormous growth in younger women entering many of the formerly male-dominated jobs, including the field of management (Social Trends, 1981). In the U.S.A., with the strongest legislation affecting the employment of women, 23.6 per cent of managers and administrators are women, followed by the U.K. with 18.8 per cent. Even so, in the U.K., the occupations in which women are most likely to be managers are traditionally female occupations such as retailing, catering and personnel. At senior levels of management there are fewer women and only 8.3 per cent of general management jobs are held by women in Britain (Training Services Division, Manpower Services Commission, 1981).

Nevertheless, the U.K. University Statistical Record shows that, from the early to late 1970s, there was a 33 per cent increase in women graduates entering industrial employment; the number of women in finance and accounting rose from 14–23 per cent in that period; in legal work from 25–32 per cent; in personnel management from 51–62 per cent; and in marketing, from 28–36 per cent.

*This chapter is based on a large-scale study sponsored by the Manpower Services Commission. We should like to thank them for their support and co-operation during this investigation, and for permission to publish this report.

This trend has been re-inforced by the increasing number of women taking university courses in management. Looking at the main universities running undergraduate courses in management in the U.K., the number rose from 187 in 1973 to 770 in 1977; as a proportion of the total management students, the percentage increased from 12–27 per cent; and in the three largest university management departments, the increase was from roughly 10–35 per cent in that same period (Cooper and Lewis, 1979). In 1981 over 40 per cent of the total management students in the largest university management department were female.

Recently, a British survey of 770 female management students found that 43 per cent believed that there was a distinct disadvantage in being a woman and desiring a career in management (Cooper and Lewis, 1979). It is of interest to note that a comparative study of female and male business graduates from the Manchester Business School found that most of the women did not reach the same level of achievement in their careers as their male counterparts. In addition, the women's salaries after graduation were, on average, only 94 per cent of the men's salaries (Crow, 1981).

While it appears easy for women to gain employment at the lower levels of the organization, it is proving very difficult for them to reach upper, middle and senior management positions. Therefore, with more women entering managerial positions, as a minority group subjected to male-dominated policy-making, research findings are indicating that female managers are subjected to a greater number of work-related pressures compared to male executives (Davidson and Cooper, 1980a; Cooper and Davidson 1982). This is of particular significance when one considers that, first, the job of management has been isolated as being a high-stress occupation for males (Cooper and Marshall, 1978; Marshall and Cooper, 1979); and second, that female managers have listed being able to 'cope with pressure' as an important factor contributing to their success (Larwood and Kaplan, 1980).

The specific problems and pressures which have been isolated as being unique to female managers include: burdens of coping with the role of the 'token woman', lack of role models and feelings of isolation, strains of coping with prejudice and sex stereotyping, and overt and indirect discrimination from fellow employees, employers, the organizational structure and climate (Hennig and

Jardim, 1979; Crow, 1981; Cooper and Davidson, 1982). These stresses on top of trying to maintain a family and/or home, are creating enormous pressures on women in management, which may manifest themselves in a variety of undesirable ways. For example, will women who take on full-time careers and those who take on traditionally male jobs (such as management) therefore join the growing number of men who suffer from stress-related illnesses as a result of work?

It is also of interest to note that two distinguished cardiologists, Friedman and Rosenman (1974), showed a significant relationship between behavioural patterns of people and their prevalence to stress-related illness, particularly coronary heart disease. Type A behaviour is characterized by 'extremes of competitiveness, striving for achievement, aggressiveness, haste, impatience, restlessness, hyperalertness, explosiveness of speech, tenseness of facial muscles, feelings of being under pressure of time and under challenge of responsibility.' Type B behaviour, on the other hand, is characterized by the relative absence of the behaviour associated with Type A individuals. On the basis of large-scale prospective research work, Rosenman *et al.* (1966) found that this Type A behaviour pattern is a significant precursor to coronary heart disease and other stress-related illnesses in all groups of people: Type A men between the ages of 39–49 and 50–59 had 6.5 and 1.9 times (respectively) the incidence of coronary heart disease than Type B men.

In this context, one interesting finding that is beginning to emerge from the Framingham Study is that working women who score high on Type A are twice as likely to develop coronary heart disease as their male Type A colleagues. Indeed, in a recent study in the U.K. carried out by the authors (Davidson and Cooper, 1980b), we found that senior female executives had significantly higher Type A behaviour scores than male executives, which in terms of the Framingham results may mean that female professional women are 'high-risk' as coronary heart disease victims.

With more women entering the male-dominated job of management in Britain, the authors decided that this was an area which required further investigation in order that pressures, problems and stress outcomes in such women were recognized and tackled. To date, research related to the problems faced by women in management has tended to be exclusively American, qualitative in nature and has concentrated on women occupying senior executive positions, i.e. the women who have overcome the barriers. Clearly, there was a need for more in-depth research, both qualitative and quantitative, in order to isolate more precisely the specific pressures being experienced by women at *all* levels of management compared to their male counterparts, and the subsequent detrimental stress outcomes.

This study provides such material since it is based on a large-scale study carried out by the authors for the Manpower Services Commission, on a large sample of female managers (across a variety of companies and industries in the U.K.), which is compared to a sample of comparable male executives. The aim of this chapter is to highlight the problem areas for both women and men managers, and to suggest ways of dealing with them (Davidson and Cooper, 1983).

METHODS

It was felt essential to adopt both a qualitative and quantitative data collection approach to this study. The qualitative approach took the form of in-depth interviews with women occupying different levels in the managerial hierarchy. The quantitative data was then obtained by formulating a survey questionnaire, based on the analysis of these interviews and previous research findings in the field.

The in-depth interviews were conducted between February 1980 and February 1981 with 60 female managers throughout England. The interviewees were made up of a stratified random sample of women occupying junior (including supervisors), middle and senior management positions, i.e. a total of 25 junior managers and supervisors, 20 middle managers and 15 senior managers. The sample was taken from a wide cross-section of private and public organizations (both male- and female-dominated). The women's positions ranged from head of firm and company directors to personnel managers, trainee marketing managers and retail supervisors.

Each tape-recorded interview lasted over one hour and covered some of the following areas: (1) potential pressures at work; (2) potential pressures at home and socially; (3) health and behaviour. Details of this material can be found in our book *High Pressure: Working Lives of Women Managers*, which was published by

Fontana in 1982.

Phase 2 of the investigation involved the development of quantitative measures in the form of a survey questionnaire. The authors' ideal main sample was to consist of a large proportion of female managers in junior, supervisory, middle and senior positions and a matched smaller sample of male managers. In addition to the different levels of management, the main questionnaire sample aimed to reflect the following four major variables:

1. A wide range of industries,
2. Small, medium and large companies,
3. Geographical variety,
4. Predominantly male/female organizations.

A random selection of 1,500 organizations throughout Britain was obtained from the following major industrial categories:

Food, Drink and Tobacco,
Chemicals and Allied Industries,
Instrument Engineering,
Electrical Engineering,
Vehicle,
Metal Goods not elsewhere specified,
Textiles,
Leather, Leather Goods and Fur,
Clothing and Footwear,
Bricks, Pottery, Glass, Cement, etc.,
Timber, Furniture, etc.,
Paper, Printing and Publishing,
Other Manufacturing Industries,
Gas, Electricity and Water,
Transport and Communication,
Distributive Trades,
Insurance, Banking, Finance and Business Services,
Professional and Scientific Services,
Miscellaneous Services,
Public Administration and Defence.

The package of questionnaires were sent to the personnel managers of these companies, each containing a covering letter, seven questionnaires and seven return stamped envelopes. The cover letter described the aims of the project and requested that the personnel officer distribute the seven enclosed questionnaires to six females and one male in their companies, occupying specified management levels.

The Main Sample

A total of 696 female and 195 male managers returned completed questionnaires. This was considered to be a good response rate taking into account that firstly, a large proportion of organizations who received questionnaire packages did not have women occupying the specified management positions and secondly, distribution of the questionnaires to respondents was dependent both on the personnel officer and permission from top management.

The female sample consisted of 26.9 per cent supervisors, 30.1 per cent junior managers, 28.4 per cent middle managers and 14.6 per cent of senior managers. Therefore, the majority of the female sample, i.e. 57 per cent occupied the lower echelons of the managerial hierarchy (i.e. supervisory and junior management positions). Conversely, only 7.6 per cent and 19 per cent of the male sample occupied supervisory and junior management positions respectively (a total of 26.6 per cent). More than twice the percentage of men occupied senior management positions, i.e. 33.7 per cent compared to the women and 39.7 per cent of males were in middle management. Ages for both females and males ranged from under 25 to over 60 years. The female managers mean age range was slightly higher than that of the men lying between the age ranges of 31–35 years and 36–40 years, as opposed to between 26–30 years and 31–35 years for males.

When comparing the average profile of the female manager respondent with her average male counterpart, there are a number of overall differences. Firstly, she is likely to be slightly older and she is less likely to be married (i.e. 56.5 per cent compared to 74.6 per cent) and more likely to be childless, and if she has children, she will have fewer children who will tend to be older. Almost twice the percentage of women managers have been divorced/separated (i.e. 15.1 per cent) compared to men managers (i.e. 8.1 per cent) and male managers are more likely to have dependants (other than children) living at home. In relation to educational qualifications, overall women managers have lower educational attainments compared to male managers, although there is little difference between the numbers having obtained university and postgraduate degrees. Conversely, female managers are more likely than male managers to have additional professional qualifications.

When looking at the overall differences in job demographics between women and men managers, the women were more likely to be concentrated in lower levels of management and supervise fewer people. In addition, the average female manager was more likely to be the first of her sex to hold the job title compared to her male counterpart. With a greater percentage of the male sample occupying middle and senior management positions compared to the female managers, it was not surprising to find that the males earned on average, a significantly higher annual salary than the females. Overall, female managers earned on average, between £6,000 and £8,000 a year compared to their male executive's salary range of between £8,000 and £10,000. Nevertheless there were strong indications that regardless of management level, men were still earning more than their female equivalents. For example, in two of the lowest annual salary ranges (i.e. under £4,000 or between £5,000 and £6,000), in *every* one of the four management level categories, there was a lower percentage of men compared to women.

However, what was particularly interesting in terms of job demographics and career pattern demographics, were some of the similarities between the female and male managers. Both female and male respondents tended to work in organizations with predominantly men in senior management, but had male and female colleagues. The majority of men and women managers had tended to have continuous work pattern profiles, although a higher percentage of women had had a break from the workforce and more female managers had, at some time, worked part-time. Both the female and male samples shared the same average 8.4 years in full-time employment in their present organization and both had been an average of 5 years in the present job. Similarities in career and job mobility patterns were further confirmed by the findings that both female and male managers had worked for an average 3.7 companies/organizations. Thus, these results suggest that women in management possess job change patterns surprisingly similar to those of their male counterparts.

Evaluation Measures

The main data collection involved the development of quantitative measures in the form of a survey questionnaire. The questionnaire was derived from previous research findings and reliable and valid measures, as well as the analysis of the interview material. The questionnaire comprised potential work/home pressures and health and behaviour measures.

Job Stressors and Management/Personality Orientation

Personal and job demographics,
Job and organizational characteristics,
Home and social characteristics,
Coping ability,
Management style,
Type A coronary-prone behaviour index.

Health/Behaviour Measures

Gurin's General Health Questionnaire,
Drug use,
Cigarette smoking,
Alcohol consumption,
Job satisfaction,
Work performance.

As the aim of the study was to ascertain the differences and similarities between female and male managers, female and male respondents were treated as two separate sub-populations of the main sample throughout the analysis. The utilization of descriptive statistical methods allowed comparisons between female and male managers. Secondly, in order to compare the statistical differences between the female and male manager samples in terms of their responses, *t*-tests were used. Finally, in order to isolate high-risk profiles of female and male managers in relation to health and behaviour measures, stepwise multiple regression analyses were used.

THE PROBLEM AREAS FOR WOMEN AND MEN MANAGERS

Figure 2.1 shows the sources of work stress that are problems for

WORK ARENA	HOME AND SOCIAL ARENA	INDIVIDUAL ARENA

Demographics

*** Lower management level
*** Lower salary
*** Fewer years worked full time
*** Discontinuous work profile
*** Greater number of years break from workforce
*** Worked part-time
*** Being first of sex to hold job title
** Larger company

Factors Intrinsic to the Job

*** Business travel and staying in hotels alone
* Having to stand on feet all day

The Token Woman

*** Lack of same sex role models
*** Sex stereotyping role imposition
*** Performance pressure

Career Development

*** Sex a disadvantage re job promotion career prospects
*** Sex discrimination and prejudice
*** Inadequate job training experience compared to colleagues of opposite sex
*** Colleagues of opposite sex treated more favourably by management

---

*** Fewer children
*** Earning more than spouse partner
*** Dependents (other than children) living at home
*** Lack of domestic support at home
*** Conflicting responsibilities associated with running a home and career
*** Being single and labelled an 'oddity'
*** Being single and sometimes excluded from social and business events

Career related dilemma concerning:

*** whether to start a family
* whether to marry live with someone
** Lack of emotional support at home
* Fewer dependents living at home

Behaviour

Management styles:

* less flexible
* Higher Type A coronary-prone behaviour scores

(continued)

| WORK ARENA | HOME AND SOCIAL ARENA | INDIVIDUAL ARENA |

Relationships at Work

*** Members of opposite
   sex seem uncomfort-
   able working with
   me because of my sex
   Experiencing
   prejudiced attitudes
   at work because of
   my sex from
   members of:
*** the same sex
*** the opposite sex
*** Feeling uncomfortable
   on training courses
   when a member of
   the minority sex
*** Sexual harassment
  ** Lack of encouragement
   from superiors
   * Lack of social support
   from people at work

STRESS OUTCOMES

Psychosomatic Symptoms

*** Nervousness, tenseness
*** Headaches
*** Tiredness
*** Difficult to get up in
   morning
*** Cry easily
*** Spells of dizziness
*** Nightmares
  ** Not eating
  ** Want to be left alone
   * Mentally exhausted

*** Total psychosomatic ill
   health score

Work Performance

*** Lack confidence in
   putting forward my
   point of view
*** Unable to be successful
*** Unable to cope well in
   conflict situations
*** Reacting too
   emotionally to work
   problems
*** Lack self-confidence
   in ability to do my
   job
   * Unable to 'sell myself'
   in competitive
   situations

  * $p < 0.05$
 ** $p < 0.01$
*** $p < 0.001$

Figure 2.1 A model of occupational stress in female managers: statistically significant higher mean scores for female managers compared to male managers

women in contrast to men managers, while Figure 2.2 indicates those that are difficulties for male as opposed to female managers. Firstly, one can quickly conclude after an examination of these figures that for both work stressor and health outcome variables, female managers reported a far greater number of significantly higher stressors compared to their male counterparts. Therefore, while all these stress precursors and manifestations were not all necessarily 'high' stressors or 'high' stress outcomes, assessed cumulatively, *women in management are experiencing higher pressure levels stemming from stressors in the work, home/social and individual arenas and more manifestations of psychosomatic symptoms and poorer work performance compared to men managers.*

In sum, the higher pressures at work to which female managers are being subjected, tend to be *stressors beyond their control, i.e. external discriminatory-based pressures.* On the other hand, this is not the case for the male manager. Significantly higher pressure scores unique to the male manager compared to his female counterpart at work, involved pressure stemming from the leadership/authority aspects of management and rate of pay (even though his salary tends to be higher than his female colleagues) (see Figure 2.2).

In the home and social arena, compared to men managers, women managers reported significantly higher pressure scores in respect of career and spouse/partner conflicts, career/home conflicts and career and marriage child-bearing conflicts. Clearly, married women managers are still not getting the required emotional and domestic support from their partners. In addition, single women managers face higher pressures than their male counterparts in relation to feeling an 'oddity', being excluded from social/business events and career conflict over whether to marry/live with someone. As well, both married and single women managers reported higher pressure over their career-related dilemma concerning starting a family in the foreseeable future.

Not surprisingly, in the individual arena, women managers had significantly higher Type A coronary-prone behaviour scores. There was only one gender difference connected to coping strategies, with men managers being less likely to talk to someone they knew in order to cope with stress. Interestingly, while there was little overall difference in the frequency with which female and male managers maintained they adopted certain management styles, certain rather detrimentally biased differences did emerge, especially for the male managers. While women managers adopted less frequently a flexible style of management; male managers reported using less frequently a flexible style of management; male managers reported using less frequently the efficient, sensitive/ sympathetic and co-operative management styles, compared to their female counterparts.

Turning to the manifestation arenas of stress, female managers reported experiencing more often, a far greater number of psychosomatic symptoms (i.e. 10), compared to men (i.e. 1), and the total mean psychosomatic ill health score was significantly higher for the female manager sample. However, male managers drank more alcohol compared to female managers. The other stress outcome concerned detrimental work performance. Unfortunately, women managers reported significantly higher detrimental work performance scores on six items compared to only one item i.e., 'unable to produce satisfactory quantity of work', scored significantly higher by men. For women managers, the poor work performance factors were predominantly associated with lack of assertion and confidence – skills which undoubtedly require emphasis in relation to future management training. After reviewing the comparative results highlighted in Figures 2.1 and 2.2, one might conclude that cumulatively, *women managers are experiencing more pressure and a greater number of stress manifestations compared to men managers.*

HIGH STRESSORS AND HIGH-STRESS OUTCOMES FOR FEMALE AND MALE MANAGERS

Figure 2.3 illustrates the high stressors* and high-stress outcomes for female and male managers in management-level terms and for each of the total samples. With the exception of Type A behaviour, demographic variables and precursor variables such as management styles, were not included. Concerning alcohol and cigarette

*A high stressor constituted a mean pressure score of 2.5 or above (1 = no pressure at all to 5 = a great deal of pressure) in response to job, organizational, home and social stressor items. The criteria selected to isolate a high-stress outcome was a mean score of 2.5 or above in response to items listed in the General Health Questionnaire, job satisfaction, the use of drugs in order to relax, and work performance measures.

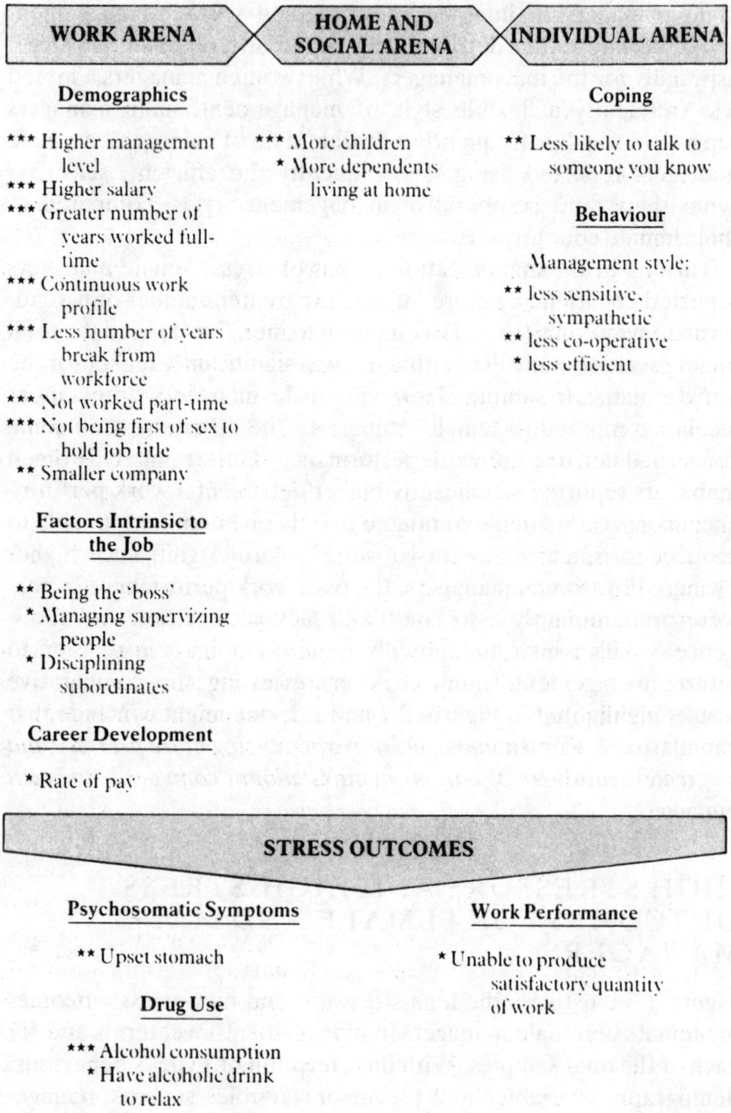

| WORK ARENA | HOME AND SOCIAL ARENA | INDIVIDUAL ARENA |

Demographics

*** Higher management
level
*** Higher salary
*** Greater number of
years worked full-
time
*** Continuous work
profile
*** Less number of years
break from
workforce
*** Not worked part-time
*** Not being first of sex to
hold job title
** Smaller company

*** More children
* More dependents
living at home

Coping

** Less likely to talk to
someone you know

Behaviour

Management style:

** less sensitive,
sympathetic
** less co-operative
* less efficient

Factors Intrinsic to
the Job

** Being the 'boss'
* Managing supervizing
people
* Disciplining
subordinates

Career Development

* Rate of pay

STRESS OUTCOMES

Psychosomatic Symptoms

** Upset stomach

Drug Use

*** Alcohol consumption
* Have alcoholic drink
to relax

Work Performance

* Unable to produce
satisfactory quantity
of work

* $p < 0.05$ ** $p < 0.01$ *** $p < 0.001$

Figure 2.2 A model of occupational stress in male managers:
statistically higher mean scores for male managers compared to
female managers

consumption, these were seen as high stress-related behaviours if the consumption rates exceeded those isolated by other researchers using comparable populations.

An inspection of Figure 2.3 reveals certain high stressors and high-stress outcomes which were common to both men and women occupying the same management level. In particular, *work overload pressures* were reported by men and women at all levels of the managerial hierarchy, with the exception of supervisors. The common high stressor for males and females occupying all the managerial levels was associated with *time pressures and deadlines*, while middle managers and supervisors of both sexes experienced high pressure due to *lack of consultation and communication*.

When it came to high-stress outcomes, females and males in senior, middle, junior and supervisory management positions, all reported smoking, drinking and eating too much; drinking coffee, coke or eating in order to relax; and (with the exception of supervisors), having an alcoholic drink as a method of unwinding. Senior female and male managers, and supervisors, most often complained of tiredness and supervisors also found it difficult to get up in the morning and wanted to be left alone. *Both male and female senior executives were highly susceptible to nervousness, feeling fidgety or tense.* Men and women in junior and middle management both seemed most at risk in relation to detrimental work performance behaviours. Junior managers of both sexes asserted that they were frequently unable to use their skills and knowledge and were unable to 'sell themselves' in competitive situations. Males and females at the middle management level maintained they frequently made mistakes at work.

An investigation into the high stressors and high-stress outcomes unique to female managers and male managers exhibited in Figure 2.3, shows that, with the exception of female supervisors, *women in junior, middle and senior management are experiencing a greater number of high stressors and high-stress manifestations compared to their male counterparts.* Moreover, female supervisors appear least 'at risk' of experiencing no unique high stressors and unlike male supervisors, being susceptible to nervousness, tenseness, headaches and making mistakes at work. *High stressors and stress outcomes specific to senior women executives involved lack of communication and consultation, Type A behaviour, wanting to be left alone, smoking cigarettes and finding it difficult to get up in the*

SENIOR MANAGERS

Females	Females and Males	Males
Lack of consultation/ communication Type A behaviour	Work overload Time pressures/deadlines	** Underpromotion

* Difficult to get up in morning Want to be left alone Smoking cigarettes	Nervousness, tenseness Tiredness Drink coffee, eat, in order to relax Smoke, drink, eat too much Have alcohol in order to relax	Making mistakes

MIDDLE MANAGERS

*** Feel have to perform better at job than colleagues of opposite sex *** Career related dilemma concerning whether to start a family *** Type A behaviour	Work overload Time pressures/deadlines Lack of consultation/ communication	* Rate of pay Sacking someone

*** Unable to cope well in conflict situations *** Tiredness * Sleep trouble * Nervousness, tenseness * Difficult to get up in morning * Want to be left alone Unable to influence and persuade people Unable to 'sell myself' in competitive situations Smoking cigarettes	Smoke, drink, eat too much Drink coffee, eat, in order to relax Have alcohol in order to relax Making mistakes	Unable to use skills and knowledge

JUNIOR MANAGERS

*** Sex a disadvantage re job promotion/ career prospects ** Office politics ** Career related dilemma concerning whether to start a family Type A behaviour Feeling undervalued Unclear career prospects	Work overload Time pressures/deadlines	** Disciplining subordinates Sacking someone Underpromotion

(continued)

Figure 2.3 High stressors and high-stress outcomes for female and male managers

Females	Females and Males	Males

Females	Females and Males	Males
*** Nervousness, tenseness *** Tiredness * Difficult to get up in morning * Want to be left alone * Unable to cope well in conflict situations Making mistakes	Smoke, drink, eat too much Drink coffee, eat, in order to relax Have alcohol in order to relax Unable to use skills and knowledge Unable to 'sell myself' in competitive situations	Unable to influence and persuade people

SUPERVISORS

Females	Females and Males	Males
	Time pressures, deadlines Lack of consultation/ communication	** Long working hours Work overload Staff shortages/turnover rate Equipment failures Unclear career prospects Rate of pay Redundancy threat
*** Nervousness, tenseness Headaches Making mistakes	Tiredness Difficult to get up in morning Smoke, drink, eat too much Want to be left alone Drink coffee, eat, in order to relax	Sleep trouble Job dissatisfaction

TOTAL SAMPLE

Females	Females and Males	Males
*** Career related dilemma concerning whether to start a family * Type A behaviour	Work overload Time pressures/deadlines Lack of consultation/ communication	Underpromotion
*** Nervousness, tenseness *** Tiredness *** Difficult to get up in morning *** Want to be left alone * Unable to 'sell myself' in competitive situations Making mistakes	* Have alcohol in order to relax Smoke, drink, eat too much Drink coffee, eat, in order to relax	

$* p < 0.05$ $** p < 0.01$ $*** p < 0.001$

morning. Undoubtedly, this latter stress outcome is linked to their complaints of tiredness which were significantly greater than senior male executives. In addition, coronary-prone behaviour pattern Type A was also an important precursor variable in middle and junior female managers – a behaviour characterized by extremes of haste, restlessness, competitiveness, impatience and feelings of being under pressure of time and under the challenge of responsibility.

There can be no doubt that middle and junior female managers reported the greatest number of combined high stressors and stress outcomes in comparison to females or males occupying any of the other managerial levels. Unlike female senior executives who have successfully broken into the higher echelons of management, middle and junior management women reported high pressure associated with sexual discrimination and prejudice, especially women in junior levels. Middle management females complained of feelings of high pressure connected with having to perform better at their jobs compared to male colleagues, and junior women managers suffered high pressure due to feeling their sex to be a disadvantage regarding job promotion/career prospects, unclear career prospects, and feeling undervalued. Junior female managers were also bothered by office politics and shared the high pressure of 'my career-related dilemma concerning whether to start a family' with female middle managers. Clearly, these results imply that *the junior woman manager views her sex as a major disadvantage in terms of her future career advancement prospects and this is a major stressor to her.*

Stress outcomes unique to both middle and junior female managers not shared with their male counterparts include nervousness and tenseness, tiredness, difficulty in getting up in the morning and wanting to be left alone. Female middle managers are susceptible to sleep troubles and tend to be heavier smokers. Both middle and junior female managers reported poor work performance behaviours not shared with their male counterparts. For middle management females these consisted of being frequently 'unable to influence and persuade people', 'unable to "sell oneself" in competitive situations', and 'unable to cope well in conflict situations'. This final poor work performance factor was also unique to junior female managers, in addition to frequently making mistakes.

In comparison to women managers, with the exception of male supervisors, there were relatively few high stressors and high-stress outcomes unique to male managers and not shared with their female counterparts. For men in senior, middle and junior management, unique high stressors tended to concern under-promotion, sacking someone, disciplining subordinates and rate of pay. Interestingly, men in these three management levels isolated one different unique detrimental performance behaviour not shared with their female contemporaries, i.e. 'making mistakes' for senior male managers; 'unable to use my skills and knowledge' for middle management males; and 'unable to influence and persuade people', for junior male managers. On the other hand, in contrast to female supervisors, male supervisors complained of a number of unique high stressors concerned with work overload and long working hours, rate of pay, staff shortages, equipment failures, unclear career prospects and redundancy threat. Unlike female supervisors, they complained of sleep troubles and were the only management category of either females or males to report high job dissatisfaction.

Looking at the total sample of male managers, a high unique stressor is related to male managers feeling they are underpromoted and employed beneath their competence (a result which would appear to confirm Harlan and Weiss' (1981) finding that male managers have higher aspiration levels than their female counter-parts). Conversely, women managers overall exhibit Type A behaviour and experience high pressure in their career-related dilemma concerning whether to start a family. They also suffer four unique psychosomatic ill health symptoms not shared with male managers, i.e. nervousness, tenseness; tiredness and difficulty in getting up in the morning; and wanting to be often left alone. They also complain of being often unable to 'sell themselves' in competitive situations and often making mistakes.

In conclusion, by summing the total high stressors and high-stress outcomes of females and males working in each of the managerial levels, it is possible to present a hierarchical list of management populations most 'at risk' in the context of 'occupational stress'. Consequently, women in junior and middle mangement experience the highest overall 'occupational stress' levels; followed by male supervisors; senior women managers; male junior managers; female supervisors and male middle managers; and finally senior male managers, who report the lowest 'occupational stress' levels. Moreover, the total female management sample reported 50 per cent more combined high stressors and high-stress outcomes in comparison to those reported by the total male management sample.

STRESS VULNERABILITY PROFILES

Stress vulnerability profiles of female and male managers most 'at risk' of showing symptoms of stress, i.e. ill health, cigarette smoking, alcohol consumption, job dissatisfaction and poor work performance; were formulated by using stepwise multiple regression analyses. From these profiles, certain general findings emerged. First, the stress vulnerability profiles of female versus male managers for each of the five stress symptoms, were on the whole, quite different. In fact, the only real similar 'high-risk' profiles of both female and male managers, was the one concerning poor work performance. Second, the strongest predictive risk variables for both female and male managers were found in the analysis of the relationships between the stressors and job dissatisfaction and detrimental work performance. Finally, it is of interest to note that, with the exception of management level and alcohol consumption, management level did not emerge as a 'high risk' predictor for any of the stress symptoms in either the female or the male management samples.

Ill Health: 'High Risk' Profiles of Female and Male Managers

The woman manager most 'at risk' in relation to psychosomatic ill health symptoms is someone who at work is subjected to high pressure associated with heavy workloads and finds carrying out job functions connected to her leadership/authority role very stressful. In addition, she often adopts a non-positive management style. At home, she is also suffering high pressure, due especially to lack of support from her partner. If she is single, she also feels the additional pressure due to being labelled a bit of 'an oddity' and being excluded from social and business functions.

The profile of the 'high-risk', illness-prone male manager is somewhat different. He is likely to have been working full-time for quite a number of years. In the work environment, he is also subjected to high work overload pressures, but also experiences high stress due to stressors related to the organizational climate and structure in which he works. He tends to feel alienated at work and frequently adopts a dogmatic style of management. Also, this male manager will have a Type A coronary-prone behaviour pattern and takes very little exercise.

Cigarette Smokers: 'High-Risk' Profiles of Female and Male Managers

The female manager who is most likely to be a heavy smoker has been in full-time employment for a great number of years and has few educational qualifications. She is probably not married, i.e. either single, divorced/separated or widowed, has a Type A behaviour pattern and will often resort to using humour as a method of relaxation.

The heavy smoker male manager, on the other hand, experiences high workload pressures, works in a small organization and experiences little stress in relation to his leadership/authority role as a manager. While his management style is often directive and co-operative, it is also non-flexible. Like female managers who smoke a lot, he is also Type A.

Alcohol Drinkers: 'High-Risk' Profiles of Female and Male Managers

The woman in management who drinks most alcohol has spent relatively few years in full-time employment and yet she has managed to work her way up quickly to the higher senior levels of management and at the same time, enjoy a high salary.

While heavy-drinking male managers also earn high salaries, unlike their female counterparts, they experience high pressures at work due to prejudice and they work in predominantly female work environments. Perhaps this finding is indicative of 'token men' in female work environments being subjected to the same prejudice pressures usually reserved for 'token women'! This male manager is likely to be unmarried, i.e. single, divorced/separated, widowed, and have a Type A behaviour pattern. The male heavy drinker is also likely to use a flexible, non-consultative but non-dogmatic supervisory style, and he rarely uses informal relaxation methods.

Job Dissatisfaction: 'High-Risk' Profiles of Female and Male Managers

The woman manager most 'at risk' in feeling high levels of job dissatisfaction is one who experiences high pressure due to stressors inherent in the organizational structure and climate in which she works. She will frequently adopt a non-positive management style at work and will tend to be quite young.

Similarly, the male manager most likely to be experiencing job dissatisfaction also suffers from high pressures linked to organizational structure and climate stressors. However, he also experiences high stress, stemming from factors intrinsic in the leadership/authority role he has to play at work. He will be earning a low salary and adopt a flexible but also non-efficient management style. Even though the dissatisfied male manager will frequently use relaxation techniques such as meditation and yoga, he will rarely talk to people or use humour as forms of relaxation. Home and social stressors have little influence on job dissatisfaction for either female or male managers. In fact, the highly dissatisfied male manager experiences very low home/partner relationship pressures.

Poor Work Performance: 'High-Risk' Profiles of Female and Male Managers

The female manager most 'at risk' in performing poorly at work is a woman feeling high pressure at work in relation to her leadership/authority role functions and from the organizational structure and climate in which she works. She frequently practices a non-positive, non-directive and non-efficient management style and is unlikely to have many (if any) children.

Likewise, the male manager most likely to perform badly at work also experiences high stress connected to leadership/authority role pressures and organizational structure and climate pressures, and he frequently adopts a non-positive management style. In addition, he tends to be non-authoritative, flexible but also non-consultative and dogmatic, in the way he manages people at work. Although he is Type A, he frequently exercises. He rarely uses humour as a form of relaxation and is likely to be unmarried, i.e. single, divorced/separated or widowed.

ORGANIZATIONAL AND POLICY CHANGES

The results from this study strongly suggest that assessed cumulatively, women managers are being subjected to far more pressures at work and at home, compared to their male counterparts. This report *is not* meant to give ammunition to any potential employers of female managers – indeed the results indicate that women who break into middle and senior levels of management have often had to be better at their job and better copers with stress than their male colleagues. In addition, there appears to be very little difference in the management styles adopted by male and female managers, if anything men maintain they use more negative management styles compared to women.

However, the disturbing findings which do emerge from this study centre on the overwhelming evidence that the *majority of additional pressures at work experienced by female managers are stressors beyond their control* and *based largely on prejudice and discrimination from both organizational/corporate policy and other people at work*. Therefore, if one takes a future prognosis of a comparative young male and female junior manager – in the majority of organizations in this country, the dice is already heavily loaded against the woman in terms of equitable salary, career development and promotions. *It is not surprising that very few women reach senior management positions in Britain.*

Many of the female managers interviewed by the authors suggested that major changes are necessary to herald 'real' equal opportunities at work. These changes will have to take into account the educational system, the socialization process, government policy and political awareness. We agree with the propositions in a report by The Industrial Society (1980) which recommended the following action: (1) stimulate industry into encouraging able women to take up careers in management and improve, therefore, attitudes among parents, teachers and women generally; (2) ensure that girls are given guidance and opportunities at schools and in higher education; (3) reduce sex bias in education and particularly in subject choice.

What is clear from our study is that the majority of organizations appear to be ensuring that management (especially higher level management) remains a *male*-dominated occupation/preserve.

Organizations have to acknowledge the fact that more women are entering management – especially at the graduate level. At the moment, *these women are not being given the same equal opportunities to develop a career in management as their male counterpart. Hence, this is an enormous loss to organizations, both in terms of economics and management talents.* It is therefore, incumbent on *all* organizations to develop corporate personnel policies that will minimize the numerous barriers, which this study has found to be particularly pertinent to women managers. It is also important that companies acknowledge the reality of dual-career managerial couples and families and accommodate them.

Thus, the following policy changes are recommended:

1. *Affirmative action* If the position of women in management in this country is to improve, we believe there is a need for stronger legislative/legalistic programmes to force equal opportunities. Britain should consider adopting the U.S. approach of 'affirmative action', whereby organizations who receive government grants or loans or contracts, etc., must follow a positive recruitment strategy toward the employment of women and minority groups or lose their government award. It is important to note that research has shown that affirmative action policies also help to change attitudes, e.g. male managers who have worked with women in senior management positions have much more positive attitudes towards women in management, compared to those who have not.

2. *Affirmative action policy and activities* We suggest that until legislative changes occur, organizations themselves should develop their own equal opportunities guidelines and affirmative action policies which provide women in management career opportunities, e.g. career planning and counselling, the creation of informal support networks for all women managers, helping male managers to come to terms with women managers and providing senior management sponsorship, etc.

   By 1978, an Equal Opportunities Commission survey of current practices of 500 leading U.K. companies revealed that only 25 per cent had formal policy statements, although most did not have associated action plans to implement them. Some companies, like ICI had surveyed their pattern of female employment and issued a code of practice to improve job appraisal and training for women, which it is anticipated may increase the number of female managers at middle and senior levels over the next few years. It is particularly important that women managers are allowed equal training opportunities, taking into account that the women managers in our study complained of inadequate job training experience compared to their male colleagues.

Organizations should follow the example of such organizations as the GLC and Thames Television which have appointed their own Equal Opportunities Committees and Advisers. Six months after the appointment of a women's employment officer at Thames Television, for example, management training to avoid sex discrimination was started. A new booklet on non-discriminatory codes of practice for interviewing has now been produced. Financial assistance for day care is now offered to male and female employees and creches are to be introduced. A company profile of staff is also being completed. Thames TV's women's employment officer is also backed by a 'positive-action committee'.

3. *Unions* Union officials should take active steps in promoting equal opportunities for women at work. Information should be requested from employers in order to assess what jobs women do. Inequalities should be researched (e.g. the survey of sexual harassment at work carried out by NALGO) and problems tackled effectively. Women should also be encouraged to stand for office in their union in order to break the male monopoly of workers' interests. In addition, Unions should consider seriously an affirmative action policy regarding the proportion of appointed female union officials.

4. *Maternity and paternity leave* With women managers at all levels of the managerial hierarchy reporting a major pressure associated with their career-related dilemma concerning whether to start a family, reasonable maternity *and* paternity leave is required, with a guaranteed right to return to work after it and with some financial security during the leave period. Paternity leave is particularly important in the changing circumstances of the family and may encourage husbands of women managers to give more emotional and domestic support in the home. In Sweden, for example, a couple is financially penalized if fathers *do not* take a minimum stipulated paternity leave. Few organiz-

ations in this country provide this contemporary innovation, but many will have to consider it in the near future if they want to deal more systematically with what may end up, if ignored, as uncontrolled absenteeism problems in the future.

5. *Day nursery facilities* The number of places in U.K. local government day nurseries were 22,000 in 1961 and only rose to 30,000 in 1980. Until governments take over the responsibility of providing day nurseries it appears that organizations will have to take the initiative themselves, by offering financial assistance for day care to both male and female employees and introducing creches.

6. *Retraining schemes* Many women who wish to return to the workforce after a number of years away, often lack confidence and feel that they are out of date. It is in the interest of employers and the wider community to provide opportunites for these women to be brought up to date with current developments. This might best be done by professional associations or indeed by work organizations providing updating courses for ex-employees who have temporarily left employment to raise a family.

7. *Flexible working arrangements* There are a wide range of flexible working arrangements that organizations can provide their female and male employees, which can help them to accommodate to changing family patterns. These include *flexi-time*, *part-time work* and *job sharing*. With the advent of the microprocessor revolution, it should also become increasingly easy for dual-career husbands and wives, in certain types of jobs, to work at home.

TRAINING IMPLICATIONS

A number of future management training implications emerge from the results of this study. It was found that 22 per cent of the interview sample were absolutely against 'female only' training courses of any kind, believing them to be a form of discrimination via segregations, arguing that it was too unlike the 'real world' in organizations. Nevertheless, the majority of this sample conceded that 'all female management training courses probably had benefits, especially for women just beginning a career in management' (see Table 2.1).

The data collected from the women manager interviewees

Table 2.1 The female managers interview sample: the training we need

Type of Training	%of Total Sample
Confidence building	50
Assertion	42
Interpersonal skills	12
General management skills including delegation, disciplining, negotiating	10
Learning to cope with men at work including sex role stereotyping imposition	8
Political awareness	7
Training for men to cope with women	6
Desocializing re: sex stereotyping	5
Leadership	5
Retraining for women entering workforce	3
Personal presentation	3
Power of speech and public speaking	3
Resilience	2
How to do well at interviews	2

supports the contention that foundation stones of social skill training were in the areas of 'confidence building' and 'being more assertive'. (The assertive person, according to Alberti and Emmons (1970) is ". . . open and flexible, genuinely concerned with the rights of others, yet at the same time able to establish very well his or her own rights".) In addition many of the women interviewed said they had benefitted more personally by attending 'off company' courses, where they were able to share work experience problems with people from different organizations as opposed to being constrained within the context of any in-company training programme.

We asked the female interviewees what managerial skills they would like to develop. Table 2.2 lists these major skills broken down by levels in the managerial hierarchy. It seems that senior female managers are more concerned with interpersonal skills of managing people, dealing with men at work more successfully as well as task skills of learning about new technology and being able to retain more information. Middle and junior managers, on the other hand, appeared to want to learn how to cope with their role as a woman manager, dealing with difficult staff (particularly men), delegation, assertiveness, being more persuasive, and supervisory managers seemed to be interested in developing the basic skills of management, such as understanding finance, new technology, administration, etc.

Table 2.2   The female manager interview sample: training skills we would like to develop

Senior Managers
Managing people generally
How to deal with men at work more successfully
Putting over a less superficial attitude – people often don't know if I mean what I say
Keeping up with new technology
Learning not to take on so much
Consulting skills
Skim reading

Middle Managers
Dealing with difficult staff, especially men
Assertion skills
Delegation
How to be taken more seriously being a woman
Disciplining

Junior Managers
Being labelled 'the boss'
Assertion and confidence
Delegation
Training abilities and assertion
Managing more people

Supervisors
Finance and budgeting
Economics
Administration
More mechanical training
More technical training

The future management training implications which emerge from the results of the larger *questionnaire survey sample*, centre largely on the types of management styles adopted by women and men managers and their detrimental work performance ratings. An examination of the 'stress vulnerability profiles' clearly illustrates the negative consequences in terms of stress outcomes when both women and men in management frequently adopt negative management styles. *Even so, it appears that overall, men managers practice negative management styles more often than their female counterparts.* While women tend to be less flexible, male managers are more likely to adopt less efficient, less sensitive and sympathetic and less co-operative management styles. Therefore, future management training for both men and women should highlight and remedy these managerial weaknesses in both sexes.

In Table 2.3, the poor work performance behaviours* for females and males in management level terms and overall, have been isolated. *Junior and middle managers* of *both sexes* report most work performance difficulties and these are mainly associated with lack of confidence, assertion and general business skills and

Table 2.3 Poor work performance in female and male managers

Females	Females and Males	Males
SENIOR MANAGERS		
		Making mistakes
MIDDLE MANAGERS		
***Unable to 'sell myself' in competitive situations	Making mistakes	Unable to use skills and knowledge
JUNIOR MANAGERS		
* Unable to cope well in conflict situations	Unable to use skills and knowledge	Unable to influence and persuade people
Making mistakes	Unable to 'sell myself' in competitive situations	
SUPERVISORS		
Making mistakes		
TOTAL SAMPLE		
*Unable to 'sell myself' in competitive situations Making mistakes	* p <0.05 ** p <0.01 *** p <0.001	

* A poor work performance behaviour constituted a mean score of 2.5 or above (1 = Never to 5 = Always) in response to the question 'How often do you feel the following at work?'.

knowledge. At the *middle management* level however, *men complain of business skill deficits*, i.e. making mistakes and being unable to use their skills and knowledge; whereas women are still maintaining they have a combination of underdeveloped business skills and confidence and assertion skills, i.e. 'making mistakes', 'being unable to influence and persuade people', and 'being unable to "sell themselves" in competitive situations'.

Senior female managers and male supervisors reported no major work performance difficulties while senior male executives and female supervisors maintained they often made mistakes. For the total male management sample, no detrimental work performance behaviours emerged constituting a mean score of 2.5 or above. On the other hand, the total female management sample reported being often 'unable to "sell themselves" in competitive situations', and often 'making mistakes'.

The results of this study clearly indicate that there is an obvious need for the introduction of more Type A behaviour modification programmes for both female and male managers. There have been fears expressed – particularly by Type A individuals – that if there are large-scale attempts to change Type A's into practicing Type B's, this will adversely affect not only the socio-economic well-being of the individuals involved, but also the country's overall quality and quantity of work output (Cooper and Marshall, 1978). However, evidence obtained from Type A behaviour modification programmes and clinical observations indicates that these fears are unfounded. Friedman and Rosenman (1974) assert that Type B individuals are just as likely to be as ambitious and intelligent as their Type A counterparts. Moreover, unlike that in Type A individuals, the Type B drive is associated with security and confidence rather than irritation and annoyance.

Type A behaviour change programmes with both coronary heart disease patients and healthy subjects have reported significant declines in serum cholesterol levels and blood pressures, lowered frequencies of subsequent coronary events, increased work productivity and improved family relationships (Chesney and Rosenman, 1980). Furthermore, Chesney and Rosenman (1980) emphasize the importance of training individuals, at the same time, to maximize their work performance.

In an attempt to change a Type A's style of living, these modification programmes involve such exercises as relaxation (both

physical and cognitive) and behavioural changes at work and home
– specific behavioural drills are introduced to be practiced in the
work environment, e.g. having fewer meetings, scheduling telephone calls, allotting free time periods and so on (Cooper and
Davidson, 1982). In addition, there is a need for both family and
friends to encourage the participant to be involved in the modification programme (Burke, Weir and Du Wors, 1979).

Finally, managers, especially women managers, must learn
techniques that help them relax, e.g. Transcendental Meditation,
breathing exercises, yoga, etc. (Cooper and Davidson, 1982).
Certainly, relaxation techniques may in the short term help the
individual prepare his/her bodily processes for the stresses and
pressures of everyday life.

Each person responds differently to stress in their environment,
as the qualitative and quantitative results from this study have
demonstrated. It is important for the woman manager to be able to
identify accurately those single or multiple related incidents that
may be causing her stress or tension.

SUMMARY OF MANAGEMENT TRAINING IMPLICATIONS

In summary, based on the overall results of our large-scale study,
we have identified the following training implications.

All Management Courses

1. *High pressure* associated with *making mistakes*, *work overload*
   and *time pressures/deadlines*, along with lack of *consultation/
   communication* are reported by both men and women managers
   from supervisors to senior executives. Managers should be taught
   to cope effectively with their workload pressures, e.g. time and
   motion exercises; learning to say 'no' to extra work, etc. In
   addition, their personal and organizational consultation and
   communication networks and systems, should be investigated
   and reappraised.
2. The *'high-risk profiles'* of both male and female managers
   isolated in this study, should be made known to all managers and
   personnel officers and utilized constructively as an aid to
   identifying and helping potentially high-risk employees in terms

of potential stress-related maladies.

3. All management training courses should highlight the potential pressures (both the similarities and the differences) faced by women and men managers at different levels of the management hierarchy. Middle and senior managers in particular, should be made aware that the majority of women in junior and middle management positions still feel *undervalued* and *discriminated against* because of their sex, in relation to future career advancement as well as performance pressure, i.e. having to perform better at their job than other male colleagues. Managers at all levels, should review and endeavour to change the situation of women managers in their own organization.

4. Mixed male and female management courses should be *specifically designed* to enable men and women to be made aware of and learn to cope with, the potential problems of working together. Managers should be taught methods of working together in harmony and as *equals*, regardless of gender. We believe that these specialized management courses are *essential in order to promote better understanding, attitude and behavioural changes*, in both male and female managers.

5. All managers should be taught to find and develop a *relaxation technique(s)* which works for them as an individual. As well, managers should be taught techniques to *modify their Coronary Type A Behaviour*.

Male Managers on Management Courses

1. Male managers need to be taught to adopt more *efficient*, more *sensitive*, *sympathetic* and more *co-operative* management styles.

2. Male manager training needs appear to be orientated towards general business skills with the exception of *junior male managers* who would particularly benefit from interpersonal skills training, including assertion/confidence skills.

3. Male managers should be taught to *cope effectively with the pressures associated with their leadership/authority role and duties*, e.g. role play situations involving disciplining subordinates, having to sack someone, etc.

4. Male supervisors appear to be the most 'high-risk' group of either male or female managers, in relation to job dissatisfaction. They complain of very specific job-related pressures,

e.g. long working hours, staff shortages, equipment failures, unclear career prospects, rate of pay and redundancy threats; and clearly require specially designed training courses. Indeed, male supervisors complain of far more work pressures than any of the other male management categories and we recommend their problems require further investigation.

Female Managers on Management Courses

1. Female managers need to be taught to adopt more *flexible* management styles.
2. Like their male counterparts, female managers require general business training skills and junior female managers in particular would benefit from learning how to cope with politics at work.
3. Women in *junior* and *middle* management would appear to benefit from interpersonal skills training with special emphasis on *assertion/confidence skills training* (a finding confirmed both by the interviews and survey questionnaires). Thus, we believe these results would tend to *support single-sex management training for women managers, especially at junior management level*, when emphasis could be made on these specific training skills. However, the problems and barriers facing women managers at work are largely due to inequality of treatment and discrimination/prejudice from organizations and male employees. Therefore, *mixed male and female management courses are also essential*, in order to expose these potential problem areas and remedy them.

In the final analysis, one cannot rely solely on legalistic approaches to equal rights, but must hope that individuals, organizations and governments can work together. This was nicely phrased by Hennig and Jardim (1979) when they said:

'Today's issue of equal employment opportunity may well be tomorrow's issue of equal rights to survival – survival as individuals, families, and corporations. If this is what we all face in our future then the need for the co-operation and coalition of employers and employees, men and women, majority and minority is clear. Ours is a joint problem which only we, together, can hope to resolve.'

REFERENCES

Alberti, R. E. and Emmons, M. L. *Your Perfect Right: A Guide to Assertive Behaviour* (Impact: London, 1970).

Burke, R. J., Weir, T. and Du Wors, R. E. 'Type A Behaviour of Administrators and Wives Reports of Marital Satisfaction and Well-Being'. *Journal of Applied Psychology*, 1979, **64**, 57–65.

Chesney, M. A. and Rosenman, R. H. 'Type A Behaviour in the Work Setting', in *Current Concerns in Occupational Stress* (Cooper, C. L. and Payne, R., eds) (John Wiley and Sons: London, 1980).

Cooper, C. L. and Davidson, M. J. *High Pressure: Working Lives of Women Managers* (Fontana: London, 1982).

Cooper, C. L. and Lewis, B. 'The Femanager Boom', *Management Today*, 1979, July, 46–7.

Cooper, C. L. and Marshall, J. *Understanding Executive Stress* (Macmillan: London, 1978).

Crow, G. 'Whither the Mistresses of Business Administration?' *Personnel Management*, September 1981, 36–9.

Davidson, M. J. and Cooper, C. L. 'The Extra Pressures on Women Executives', *Personnel Management*, 1980a, **12**, 6, 48–51.

Davidson, M. J. and Cooper C. L. 'Type A Coronary-Prone Behaviour and Stress in Senior Female Managers and Administrators', *Journal of Occupational Medicine*, 1980b, **22**, 801–6.

Davidson, M. J. and Cooper, C. L. *Stress and the Woman Manager* (Blackwell: Oxford, 1983).

Friedman, M. and Rosenman, R. H. *Type A Behaviour and Your Heart* (Wildwood House: London, 1974).

Harlan, A. and Weiss, C. Moving Up: Women in Managerial Careers, unpublished paper, (Wellesley College: Boston 1981).

Hennig, M. and Jardim, A. *The Managerial Woman* (Pan Books: London, 1979).

Industrial Society *Women in Management – Onwards and Upwards?* (Industrial Society: London, 1980).

Larwood, L. and Kaplan, M. 'Job Tactics of Women in Banking', *Group and Organization Studies*, 1980, March, vol. 5, 1, pp. 70–9.

Marshall, J. and Cooper, C. L. *Executives Under Pressure* (Macmillan: London, 1979).

Rosenman, R. H., Friedman, M. and Strauss, R. 'CHD in the Western Collaborative Group Study', *Journal of the American Medical Association*, 1966, **195**, 86–92.

Social Trends (HMSO: London, 1981).

Training Services Division, MSC *No Barriers Here? – A Guide to Career Development Issues in the Employment of Women.* (HMSO: Leicester, 1981).

3 Choices for women managers
Sandra Langrish–Clyne

INTRODUCTION

This chapter arises from my involvement over a five-year period with the development of training programmes for prospective and aspiring women managers. This group of women has included those employed at the lowest level of responsibility in organizations (e.g. supervisors, charge-hands) who would usually be unlikely to rise to a higher level, and young graduate trainees, supposedly being 'groomed for stardom' but in reality experiencing considerable frustration and difficulty through being blocked from attaining responsible positions.

The training programmes were intended to provide some of the skills and knowledge which they needed to assist them in attaining promotion and more responsible management posts. A preliminary research study, funded by MSCs was carried out to identify their training needs (Langrish and Smith, 1979), and this was followed by further grants from MSC to develop and conduct an exploratory and experimental series of training programmes (Langrish and Smith, 1981), culminating in the production of a manual of training materials in modular form (Smith *et al.*, 1983) which can be used by organizations to design and conduct their own training.

The design and content of the programmes was based upon American experience and our own research findings and focussed upon four major areas of skills and knowledge. These were:

knowledge of management and business,
inter-personal skills training,
self-assessment and career planning,
women in management.

The content was amended and developed through successive programmes with changes of emphasis and additions and deletions in the light of experience.

The non-residential programme was divided into three one-week blocks separated by periods of about nine weeks during which time participants returned to their jobs, spending a half to one day a week conducting in-company projects.

Judging by the objective evaluation of the courses which was carried out and the participants' subjective comments, the courses were 'a success' although a number of participants recognized that they might not be able to apply all they had learnt on the courses when they returned to their companies. Follow-up of participants revealed that a number had changed jobs within their organization or moved to new jobs, received additional development and training or even achieved some promotion. So, on the face of it, our courses appeared to have had a positive effect upon their careers, although of course it is almost impossible to say whether these changes might have occurred anyway without our intervention.

But reflecting on the programmes during their planning and implementation and after, it occurred to me that we may have been ignoring some important questions about the wider effects upon their lives and have been basing the courses upon some un-questioning and unreasonable assumptions. It is these questions and assumptions together with what is known about women managers' lives that I wish to explore further.

Amongst others the most significant and fundamental question concerned the issue of *choice* in their lives. Were we opening up greater choice and control of their own lives or were we channelling them into an ever-narrowing series of options? Face value suggested greater choice and control, but perhaps they were being encouraged to exercise this capacity within a limited and limiting context.

Although problems and barriers were explored they were examined from within a set of unstated and unchallenged assumptions, the most important of which seemed to be that women:

should get a better deal from employment in terms of the job they

do, their pay and other rewards, and the satisfactions of work,
have as a group as much potential to achieve and be successful at
work as men,

are as capable as men at succeeding in positions of responsibility in
whatever field of employment they may choose,

would gain substantial rewards both material and in terms of
personal fulfilment by having managerial jobs,

can be assisted in achieving these positions and their rewards by
special training and preparation,

can be as successful as men at succeeding in male-defined structures
(most organizations) if they have special preparation.

If all these are true, then,

women should enter management and receive special training to
help them to be successful.

Hence, the proliferation of courses both in the U.S.A. and
increasingly in this country also. Although this conclusion may
appear to be the obvious corollary of the previous assumptions,
closer examination of the reality of women's training and the values
which it supports and women's lives as managers may lead to a
different conclusion.

Amongst the most important questions to be examined in this
paper are:

What is known about women managers?

What is the effect of organizational factors upon women managers?

What is women's management training and development telling
them?

How is it possible to increase women managers' choices?

We begin by looking at some of the research on women
managers.

WHO ARE THE WOMEN MANAGERS? – THEIR CHARACTERISTICS

Estimates of the numbers of women managers in the U.K. vary
from 9 per cent (Cleverdon, 1980) to 15 per cent (Alexander, 1979).
Of these, less than 1 per cent of women managers operate at Board
level (Melrose-Woodman, 1978). However, in the U.S.A. the

figure is much higher, with about 25 per cent of women managers and administrators.

The term 'women managers' embraces a heterogeneous rather than a homogeneous group. It is composed not only of women who have risen to senior positions and held these posts for many years, but also women who have risen from fairly subordinate positions to obtain a post of some responsibility but will never make the top, plus the new generation of young graduate high flyers who have set their sights upon the most senior jobs. There is also a further group known as 'aspiring' or 'potential' women managers who have not yet achieved a position of responsibility, but would like to do so.

The characteristics of women managers have been of interest to researchers for a number of years and a number of studies have been carried out. In terms of their family background, Almquist (1974) and Vogel et al., (1970) found that women who chose non-traditional careers (such as management) were raised in families where the mother worked full-time. Hennig and Jardim (1977) have shown that it is important for successful women managers to have had a close relationship with a father who encouraged non-female stereotypical behaviour and self-concepts. Place (1979), in a study of senior female managers in New Zealand, found that although most of their mothers were not employed outside the home, they had successful fathers and both parents were considered to be supportive of their career choice.

Studies of 'pioneers' (women whose career goals were in predominantly masculine fields) have shown that this group were more likely than 'traditional' women to marry later, to have fewer children and have them later in life and return to work earlier after their birth (Rossi, 1967; Almquist and Angrist, 1971; Hennig and Jardim, 1977). Recent studies (Brown, 1979; Harlan, 1978) confirm that women managers are only a third to a half as likely as male managers to be married and less likely to have children.

The most recent study of the characteristics of women managers in the U.S.A. confirms these findings (Korn Ferry International, 1982). Their survey of 300 top women managers found that only 49 per cent were married (compared with 95 per cent of male managers), a quarter had never married and a fifth were divorced or separated. Only a third of this group had children, compared with 97 per cent of men in equivalent jobs. Gutek et al. (1981) have suggested that women managers may choose to avoid the conflicts and problems of dual-career relationships by remaining single. This has led to the popular and possibly stereotypical picture of women in middle and senior managerial posts as dedicated single and single-minded 'career women'. There is some truth in the picture of older, established senior women as 'Queen Bees' (Staines *et al.*, 1974), who have had to fight their way through the organization and as a result may regard themselves as something apart and jealously guard their uniqueness by discouraging or even excluding younger aspiring women. Instead of easing the path of their younger women colleagues to more senior positions by acting as their mentor, they may show active hostility and resentment.

They may, of course, be married (although this is less likely) in which case they are likely to cultivate the 'superwoman' image by succeeding not only at a high level job but also running a home and a family. However, this ability to succeed in two worlds is unlikely to make them any more receptive to new young up-and-coming women. They are likely to say to themselves, 'I had it hard and I managed – why should I make it easy for them?'

This picture illustrates one important effect that being a senior manager may have upon these women's lives. In order to get on they have had to make sacrifices in their personal lives as well as making themselves acceptable to men in organization. The greatest compliment she can be paid is that she 'thinks like a man', whilst at the same time trying to retain her 'femininity'. She often has low regard of 'other women' who according to popular wisdom are 'scatter-brained', overly emotional, irrational and undependable (Pogrebin, 1976). She has thrown in her lot with men and, as a consequence has had to deny many female qualities which would have enriched both herself and the organization.

Additionally, she creates a problem for new bright young women graduate entrants for whom she presents not only a barrier, but also a negative image.

This group of young women has emerged primarily as the result of the increasing number of girls in higher education. Traditionally, girls have preferred arts/social science options and have rejected science/technology and numeracy specialisms which lead to a range of jobs in traditionally masculine fields. They have also tended towards the caring professions and rejected the hard world of business and commerce. However, there is some indication that this view is changing slowly. In the Department of Management

Sciences at UMIST there has been an increasing number of girl students over the last five to ten years and the figure now stands at about 40 per cent of the total intake. In addition, the girls tend to get a disproportionate number of Firsts and special prizes awarded for outstanding performance during their degree studies. This trend is confirmed by figures produced by the American Assembly of Collegiate Schools of Business (AACSB) which has shown women taking up to 40 per cent of places on Business School courses (Fox, 1977; Robertson, 1978).

Does this mean that there is likely to be a concomitant increase in the numbers of women managers emerging from this group during the next decade or two? Some comparative research on the attitudes and values of male and female management students at UMIST has shown that the girls see the successful career woman as their most favoured life choice with the boys favouring the traditional role of husband and father who also has a career. This suggests that the stereotypical pattern of the unmarried single-minded career woman will be perpetuated in the present generation. But this view has to be moderated by further research amongst this group which indicated that the girls saw themselves as following (reluctantly) the more traditional pattern of marriage and family with a career fitted in when and how they were able. Given their initial high ambition and wish for success and independence, this group is faced with some hard choices in trying to reconcile traditional roles with the less traditional option of career success allied with marriage and children.

Cooper (1982) suggests that the stresses for career women of maintaining the dual roles of corporate manager and family manager will mean either that an increasing number will choose to stay single or that men will have to accept a greater share of responsibility for maintaining family support systems. The problems for women of their dual managerial role has had the effect of increasing the levels of psychological and physical ill health amongst them (Cooper and Davidson, 1981; Cooper, 1980).

It is clear therefore that women managers are faced with difficult decisions in reconciling their work and personal lives. Conflicts of this kind exist for all working women and particularly married women with children but they impact particularly strongly upon women managers because of the demands of the job. The most important question is the extent to which they are aware of the price they may have to pay in achieving more responsible posts and whether this is balanced by the rewards. Each woman must arrive at her own individual decision about balancing this difficult equation, but it must be done through a thorough understanding and knowledge of personal costs and benefits.

There is certainly ample evidence that women have the ability to be managers, although the nature of their contribution may be subject to discussion. For example, in a recent study Moore and Rickel (1980) examining the characteristics of women in traditional and non-traditional managerial roles found that non-traditional groups were more achieving, emphasized production more and saw themselves as having characteristics more like managers and men.

This raises, however, the important question of whether women managers should aspire to be 'like managers and men' or whether they have unique 'female' qualities to contribute to improve the quality and effectiveness of organizational life. Von Boeschoten (1983) takes the view that if this happened, there would be more time and interest for people, more commonsense approaches based on human realities, rather than abstract logical ideas, and opportunity to give expression to their full human capacities. This view enters the arena of debate on 'right-brain/left-brain' capacities (Gazzaniga, 1970, 1978). The left brain is thought to be responsible for logical, analytical abstract thought, the right brain the creative, imaginative, feeling and emotional side of our natures. It is becoming increasingly the view that the left brain (primarily masculine values) has achieved a disproportionate domination of our thought and action as human beings and that to achieve a balanced and full expression of human capacities we should begin to acknowledge, value and use our right brain as well. However, the evidence suggests this is unlikely to happen.

This has considerable implications for women managers. If, as appears to be the case, most organizations and men managers are left brain-dominated, what happens to women who work in these organizations and are called upon to work mainly as left brain people? They may go along with it and ignore their right brain capacities or demonstrate right brain-dominated abilities and be seen to have all the pejorative characteristics ascribed to women. In either case, there is likely to be considerable conflict and discomfort in reconciling conflicting modes of thought and action.

WOMEN IN ORGANIZATIONS

There are a number of additional factors affecting whether women may fit into traditional organizational systems. These are primarily:

company systems and practices,
male managers' attitudes towards and perceptions of women managers.

The company systems which may bar women from responsible positions operate at two levels: the entry level and the progression to managerial jobs. At the entry level, women are likely to be less well qualified than men and as a result may be excluded from certain positions (Stein, 1976). Personnel systems such as selection may be used to inhibit rather than facilitate the progress of women and the 'career path' factor, which is designed to fit the life pattern of men rather than women, ensures that women are prevented from progressing through the organization (Ashridge, 1980).

This finding is confirmed by Snell *et al.* (1981) who identified 'jobs and promotion' criteria acting as further barriers to women in addition to those set up by attitudes to women at work and structural, organizational and industrial factors.

Bias against women in both the selection and treatment of female managers has been found in a number of studies. Dipboye *et al.* (1975) found significant effects of applicant sex (favouring males) in management selection decisions of both university students and professional recruiters. Terborg and Ilgen (1975) found that students asked to allocate starting and second-year salaries to a male and female with the same qualifications and performance record recommended a significantly higher level of compensation for males than for females. Rosen and Jerdee (1974), in a study of the attitudes of Harvard Business Review subscribers, found a bias against women in management, promotion, and development and Cecil *et al.* (1973), provide evidence that different variables are used to evaluate male and female job applicants. Schwartz (1971), in a study of top executives, showed that the majority of respondents felt that women had less motivation, were not a good investment and were not as committed to their careers as men. Differential treatment of women in selection has been reported by Fidell (1970) and Shaw (1972), in promotion policies (Day and Stogdill, 1972; Kanter, 1977) and in segregation into 'women's jobs' (Alvarez and Lutterman, 1979).

One suggested explanation for this is the assumption that women lack the qualities considered to be required of a manager, such as aggression and leadership qualities (Bond and Vinacke, 1961; Maier, 1970; Megaree, 1969). In a study that sought managerial opinions about women executives, Bowman *et al.* (1965) showed that male respondents agreed that women are 'temperamentally unfit for management'.

In addition, senior executives may provide covert discrimination against women in the form of 'kindly protective attitudes . . . concerning the "real" interests and abilities of women and the types of work for which they are most suited' (Ashridge, 1980).

The effect of these attitudes upon women's selection and promotion is to make it very difficult for them to progress through the organization. There may be important issues about taking a break to have children and risking getting off the career ladder, or if no break is taken, a woman may find her promotion prospects blocked anyway through men managers' resistance to the entry of women into management.

Alpert (1976) explains men managers' resistance to the entry of women into management by identifying a double standard in the expectations of the roles of men and women managers. Men are permitted to play two separate roles, one at home and one at work, but women's work, in contrast, is commonly transferred from home to the office and added on to the job function. This has the effect of confusing male managers when they're faced with women behaving in a 'masculine' or 'non-feminine' way by asking for a rise or promotion. It also explains women's placement in staff or service functions, rather than operations, industrial sales or other line functions. Bass *et al.* (1971) suggest that male managers have learnt to relate to 'traditional' women and have come to expect this behaviour amongst working women and so experience difficulties with women who do not defer to them or who expect equal treatment on the same basis as men.

The sources of male managers' bias against women managers may lie in the sex stereotyping of management as an occupation which requires 'masculine' characteristics which women are not thought to possess.

The existence of a 'male managerial model' has been established by a number of investigators. O'Leary (1974) confirms that it is the male, not the female sex role stereotype which coincides with the managerial model which is one of independence, objectivity, task orientation and aggressiveness (Terborg and Ilgen, 1975; Bartol, 1976). These characteristics, which comprise a 'competency' cluster, include such attributes as problem-solving and decision-making ability, are believed to be important in management and to be the prerogative of the male. This is contrasted with a 'warmth-expressiveness' cluster ascribed to the female population (O'Leary, 1974).

In addition to the problems outlined above there, is a further important issue which is concerned with the nature of organizations and the place of women within them.

PUBLIC WORLD, PRIVATE WORLD

Historically, the public sphere has been assigned to the male and the private sphere to the female. The public arena is one in which 'real work' is carried out and the private arena exists to maintain and support the activities of those who are active outside in the public domain. Different qualities are required to be successful in these two worlds. The outer world requires independence, rationality and self-reliance; the inner private world demands dependence, emotionality and support. It is easy to see that because men inhabit the public world they are assigned the characteristics needed (masculine) and women, the private world and female characteristics. Hence they are seen to lack the necessary characteristics of a manager.

There is considerable evidence that this division of public and private, outer and inner and defined in the minds of men, particularly, as 'important' and 'unimportant' is good neither for women, nor people in general. The requirements of the public sphere work to the disadvantage of men who also have emotional needs which they are required to deny, and relegate women to the private and 'unimportant' sphere which prevents them from contributing to the outer 'real' world.

The difficulty of uniting the public and private spheres means that women entering the work-force as professionals are neither expected nor understood there. Therefore their status is that of 'outsider' (Forisha, 1981) in a place in which they do not belong. Kanter (1977) observes that under these circumstances women are given the status of bitch, witch, pet or doll or alternatively are cloaked in invisibility and lack of recognition. Women may not want to remain on the outside, with all its attendant lack of recognition and lack of reward, but neither do they want to behave like imitation men, as an imitation is never quite as good as the real thing. They may respond by under-achieving, or alternatively may compensate by over-achievement either by being very good at things they consider will get them recognition and approval (e.g. efficiency), or begin to act like stereotypical females or imitation males. However, some women *do* succeed. Anderson (1974) considers that the qualities required for success are those which allow them 'to cope emotionally with being reacted to as a deviant'. They must not only demonstrate their competence but learn the behaviour which will change the image of working women in the minds of both men and women (Fuller and Batchelder, 1953), a daunting task, indeed.

Forisha (1981) considers that this can only be done by individual initiative combined with collective efforts with other women. If women are successful there will be integration of the masculine and feminine, of the inner sphere and the outer, and that everyone, both men and women will benefit. But there is little evidence that organization structures are inclined to be receptive to this kind of change. They are more likely to seek stability in forms established by the social structure (Hampton-Turner, 1970).

The reason for this lies in the nature of the exercise of power in organizations. Many organizational theorists have examined the nature of power in organizations. Organization structures are based on power and men are adept at utilizing it to meet their personal and organizational needs. Women, more accustomed to being less direct and more covert in their use of power, may not understand the nature of power in organizations which requires meeting group norms, building formal and informal networks and playing the organizational game by male rules.

The effective use of power encourages ambition and develops self-confidence. The corollary is that powerlessness blunts and reduces feelings of being in control of self and one's personal environment. Becoming accustomed to being the Boss requires the development of skills which are on the masculine side of the continuum of male/female characteristics. Training for women managers has encouraged and fostered the development of such skills as assertiveness and negotiation skills which are presented as alternatives to becoming 'like men' whilst at the same time covertly telling women that they can be like men, as long as it is well disguised.

The impact of these factors upon women managers' training will be explored in the following section.

TRAINING FOR WOMEN MANAGERS: A LOOK AT THE CONVENTIONAL WISDOM

In the United States, the development of training for women managers began in the 1970s and in many respects has provided a model for this country. Much of the material included in training courses was pioneered by the Women's Colleges of Simmons, Wellesley and Bryn Mawr who first designed courses exclusively for women managers.

Recently, interest in this field in the U.S.A. has led to the publication of popular books which give advice and guidance on 'how to make it in management'. A typical example of this genre is *Women Executives in a Changing Environment* (Fenn, 1979), a book designed to 'encourage women to expand their repertory of behavioural responses as managers and to risk growth, development, and the use of strategy for one's career' (p. xiv). She suggests that the key words for women who are moving ahead are 'competence, confidence and credibility' (p. 1) and goes on to explore these themes through an examination of sponsorship (mentors), power, inter-personal skills and conflict. Nowhere does she question what developing these skills may mean in terms of their total life experience and the personal costs of this development. The underlying philosophy is succeed and don't question the cost.

An even more extreme view is taken by Landau and Bailey (1980) in *The Landau Strategy: How Working Women Win Top Jobs*. This book is a manual on planning success, promoting and packaging yourself and 'making your sale' (of yourself). Words such as 'gruelling', 'exhilarating', 'orchestration' and 'hard-nosed' abound. Once again there is total acceptance of the philosophy of success as the name of the game.

Although these books, and many others like them, present an extreme picture of the underlying assumptions and philosophy of women's management development, such attitudes, in a much gentler and more low-key way, pervade much of women's management training today.

Included amongst the most popular forms of training is assertiveness training. This seeks to make women more assertive by helping them to distinguish between aggressive, assertive and non-assertive behaviour and to assist them in applying these concepts by using rehearsal and role-play to bring about a change in behaviour. Although this training was not developed exclusively to meet the needs of women (Smith, 1975; Alberti and Emmons, 1970) it has been adopted enthusiastically and become one of the most frequently incorporated elements in women managers' development programmes.

What is this training saying to women? On the surface it is saying 'this is how to become acceptable as managers'. But is it really saying, 'this is how to soften your approach in order to be acceptable to men managers? After all, it doesn't pay to appear to be too powerful'.

In training courses, particular emphasis is placed upon knowledge of management and business, in order to understand the rules of the management game. This accords with the philosophy of the books mentioned earlier. Know your enemy, learn the rules, and you may get a lollipop in the form of promotion, if you're lucky.

Additionally, having a sponsor or mentor to help your career along is also frequently mentioned in the context of succeeding as managers. This role may be taken by either a woman or a man, and is intended to facilitate learning the rules of the management game through someone who has already succeeded. To paraphrase an early advertising slogan, 'If you want to get ahead, get a mentor'. As Fenn (1980) says 'Progress in a career requires access to inner circles of associations that are difficult to attain. Elite positions in organizations have traditionally been reserved for men. If women are to function effectively as organization members, they need access to inner circle support . . . women who are serious about a career are beginning to discover that it is possible to enhance credibility through sponsorship' (pp. 24, 25). But to what extent does this mean 'selling out' to organizational (i.e. male) norms and values?

However, it is also acknowledged that women need to develop their own networks. As well as gaining access to existing groups within organizations it is recognized that women need to develop their own networks. In, *Is Networking For You? A Working Woman's Alternative to the Old Boy System*, Stern (1981) describes the basic principle of networking in the process of gaining jobs or access to power as '*Who do you know?*'. Networks may be *internal* (organization-based), *external* (industry-based), or *personal* (people I have known/know now). The benefits of networking include

being able to call on others' expertise,
being on an external grapevine through which information is passed,
being already known to those with power to help,
being in a position to seek out new contacts more easily (Smith, K., 1983).

Professional networks (e.g. Women in Banking, Women in Engineering, Women in Personnel) have proliferated in the U.K. during the last few years. Involvement in such groups, and the creation and development of personal networks both inside and outside the organization are said to have enabled members to expand and enlarge their spheres of influence, knowledge and power. Most groups meet in London at regular intervals (usually monthly) and have a programme of speakers and seminars on topics of interest to members. The style of these gatherings is said to be relaxed, informal and open and usually lacks the constitutional and administrative procedures and constraints that are apparent in the more formalized male-determined professional bodies.

It is apparent that such networks fulfil an important need. The question is the extent to which they operate effectively to achieve the benefits listed earlier or whether they become forums to play well-established Transactional Analysis games such as 'Ain't It Awful!' There is certainly 'sharing' but to what end? If such networks are to become centres of power and influence they may have to abandon the rather 'cosy' mode of operation they have at present and become more 'hard-nosed'. Of course, in doing so, they will once again be adopting the 'male' style discussed at some length earlier and fail to be uniquely female, but if they don't, they may fail to achieve their objectives – damned if you do, damned if you don't. Once again, women may be faced with difficult choices.

Certainly establishing internal networks is bound to encounter resistance, both overt and covert from the organizational hierarchy and from individual women and men, and may appear to be highly threatening to existing norms and power structures.

One kind of seminar for women managers which is particularly useful in opening up issues of personal choices for women managers as well as all employed women and those contemplating employment is the life-planning workshops. In these, women are given the opportunity to carry out vocational planning within the framework of one's whole life and evaluate and plan choices for the future. Assessment of past and present performance and achievements, present circumstances, plus an examination of personal strengths and weaknesses gives an opportunity to plan short-term and long-term goals in both work and personal life in order to achieve a balance of satisfactions.

Although much of the women managers' training is based upon the assumption that 'success' must be the goal, life-planning workshops are essential if such work-oriented goals are to be incorporated into women's total life experience in a way which will increase their satisfaction rather than add to their stresses.

It is impossible to consider women managers' training without a brief look at training for men managers responsible for women subordinates. This section has to be brief as there has been relatively little attention paid to the importance of preparing men managers for working with ambitious women.

A number of writers have suggested that there is a considerable need for training for men managers, although it is acknowledged that it may be difficult to persuade men of this need and for them to be prepared to participate in such training. Huffmire (1976) and Macdonald (1979) have identified a need for awareness training for men to assist women to realize their potential and that these should include an examination of commonly prevailing myths about women managers. Kozoll (1973) suggests that there should be seminars to identify negative reactions to women in professional roles and to identify work strategies to combat them. Herbert and Yost (1978) emphasize the need to educate male managers in the need for development programmes for women to prepare them for management responsibility.

Although, in many important respects, men managers hold the key to the entry of women managers to positions of increased responsibility and seniority it may be women managers' task to ensure that opportunities are created and utilized, as it is unlikely that men managers will do so voluntarily.

Most training available to women managers is based upon the assumption that *of course* you all want to get on, and here's how to do it. The barriers and problems inevitably encountered are recognized and women are instructed in how to get over them, round them or under them. The large amount of effort and hard work required is acknowledged but is considered to be an acceptable price to pay for the rewards and benefits on offer.

Lorraine Paddison, former Director of the Women Managers Research Training Programme at Ashridge Management College, writing in the Spring 1983 edition of the NOWME Newsletter, acknowledges how difficult she has found entering the world of banking and finance even though she had had a number of years' experience researching the place of women managers in organizations. If *she* has had problems, what is likely to be the experience of women managers without her considerable awareness and experience of the problems to be encountered?

Working as a woman manager in a traditional setting is difficult for women, but the rewards are considerable. Is it possible for women to obtain these rewards in any other way? This question will be considered in the next section.

IN SEARCH OF ALTERNATIVES

One important alternative to working as a manager in a large organization is that of becoming an entrepreneur and starting your own business. Sexton and Kent (1981) have reported a comparative study of female executives and entrepreneurs which indicates that they tend to have similar characteristics, with the dominant work motivation being job satisfaction and professional recognition. This is consistent with McClelland's (1969) finding of a higher need for achievement (n. ach.) among entrepreneurs than in the general population, but it is interesting that it is also found in this sample of female executives.

Some differences were apparent, notably that the female executives thought working with people was the key ingredient for success and the entrepreneurs saw persistence as the key. Both groups saw themselves as 'doers' but the executives interpreted this as being 'managers' and 'organizers' whereas the entrepreneurs saw themselves as 'planners' and 'promoters'. However, both groups indicated high propensity for risk-taking, a significant characteristic of entrepreneurs (Komives, 1973). The authors conclude that 'Much of the mythology surrounding female entrepreneurs and how they are different from female executives is not supported by this study'.

The impulse to begin a new business venture has been identified by Roberts (1968) as frustration with lack of support in their previous organizational job resulting in a search for greater autonomy and scope for their talents by founding their own companies. This may be significant for women similarly frustrated by lack of both promotion and responsibility in management jobs.

Although most of the research on female entrepreneurs has been carried out in the U.S.A., Watkins and Watkins (1983) have reported the first results of a study of female entrepreneurs in the U.K. Their demographic analysis shows that the women were ill-prepared by their education and work experience to be successful in their own business but that they had 'a strong motivation to autonomy and achievement', a finding which supports Sexton and Kent's (1981) results from the U.S.A.

The need for preparation for success in small business has been recognised for some time in the U.S.A. and is beginning to be so in this country also. Entrepreneurship training is considered to create an opportunity for consideration of this career option in an enlightened fashion and to offer the management skills and experience needed to improve the chances of entrepreneurial success.

In the U.S.A. this process may begin in schools with career education to build awareness of self-employment as an acceptable option for employment (Flexman, 1980). A number of programs designed to assist children to explore the problems to be solved in business have been introduced in a number of schools and Bottom Line: Unequal Enterprise in America (1978) calls for local communities to join forces in increasing options for young females. Materials intended to help teachers and counsellors have been designed by Dr. Thomas Scanlon of the University of Illinois for developing skills in eight personal competency areas necessary for successful entrepreneurship. These are:

planning and goal-setting,
decision-making,
inner control,
risk-taking,

innovation,
human relations,
reality perception,
feedback usage.

These are used in career guidance courses for young student groups. In addition, Carol Kaplan (American Institute of Research) has developed six modules using a competency-based approach to entrepreneurship skill training which may be readily integrated into traditional class-room experiences.

Opportunities for specialized training offered by the Small Businesses Association (SBA) in the U.S.A. have been enthusiastically grasped by women with almost 80,000 attending courses in 1977, increasing in a single year (1979) by 65 per cent to 130,000. Two-day pre-business workshops were offered by the SBA, followed by a 45 hour competency-based curriculum package. The Women Business Owners Orientation Program offers women (and men) the skills needed to start, buy and expand a small business. An added benefit to the WBO program is the network that builds among the participants leading after the first six months of 1981 to the establishment of 143 network institutions who have banded together to improve the quality and quantity of short-term small business training. Over 12,000 persons, of whom 50 per cent are women, have enrolled in one or more of the courses and workshops offered by the network institutions.

Another approach has been developed by the Women Entrepreneurs Project based at the University of California during 1977–78 which has led to a popular book called *Be Your Own Boss* (McCaslin and McNamara, 1980). Shapero (1980) advocates the use of case studies of successful women entrepreneurs and outstandingly successful women who can act as role models.

Career counselling for women is advocated by Smith *et al.* (1977) who suggest that counsellors should have:

awareness that women need special training/education to overcome education deficits in special areas such as maths,
skills in 'selling' to women the appropriateness of certain careers viewed previously as the male domain,
insights into methods of learning how to reconcile personal and career goals,
assertiveness training applied to assertive career pursuit,

empathy for students experiencing discriminatory barriers in non-traditional careers.

The authors recognize the possibility of role stress and or role overload confronting the youthful female exploring small business ownership. Short-term training seminars have been developed and marketed by Carol J. Harnon, President of Turnstyle Inc., a personnel management firm based in Tulsa, Oklahoma. Her seminars focus upon:

building memory skills to improve communication,
basic management principles allied to the development of a
    personalized management style,
goal-setting and time-management,
decision-making and problem-solving techniques,
methods of building self-esteem whilst coping with stress.

Many of these elements would be included in management programmes for men managers and are not uniquely needed by women entrepreneurs. However, they do highlight the parallel, mentioned earlier (Sexton and Kent, 1981), between management and entrepreneurship.

The advantages of small business entrepreneurship over being a woman manager in a large organisation is primarily that it increases the element of choice in women's lives. Instead of struggling with the problem of being accepted by men managers as competent, capable and promotable, she can carry out self-assessment and personal development within her own terms without having other people's norms and stereotypes thrust upon her.

There is also the possibility of greater flexibility in terms of job time-tabling enabling her also to avoid the conflicts of marry/not marry, children/no children. It is acknowledged that to become a successful entrepreneur requires a devotion and single-mindedness which may appear to contradict the idea of flexibility, but she has the choice of how much effort she wishes to put into the business, compared with other areas of her life.

The choice of business, the management style she adopts, the style and size of the organization are also within the realm of personal choice and temperament. She can exercise and develop her ability as a manager with its attendant satisfactions without sacrificing other, equally important aspects of her life.

Until work is re-structured in such a way that the standard 9–5,

48-week working year is no longer the norm, women in small-business ownership may be the new pioneers of employment opportunities for women.

There is a wealth of experience and ideas of training and preparation for entrepreneurship for women in the U.S.A. which may be adopted and adapted in a similar way to training for women managers during the 1970s and 1980s. At the moment, only the Manchester Business School is pioneering this approach, and it may develop into the new growth area for women managers of the 1980s.

As an alternative to being a manager in someone else's business, managing your own business can give women an escape route from the stresses of corporate jobs. Goffee *et al.* (1982) reporting a study of 50 women entrepreneurs in the U.K. conclude that: 'during the present economic recession . . . more women may well opt for self-employment and small-scale proprietorship'.

Could this be the way ahead for many women?

REFERENCES

Alberti, R. E. and Emmons, M. L. *Your Perfect Right: A Guide to Assertive Behaviour* (Impact, 1970).

Alexander, M. C. R. 'Equal opportunities and vocational training. Training and labour market policy measures for the vocational promotion of women in the U.K, unpublished paper, (*CEDEFOP*: Berlin, 1979).

Almquist, E. M. Sex stereotypes in occupational choice: the case for college women, *Journal of Vocational Behaviour*, August 1974, **5**, no. 1, 13–21.

Almquist, E. M. and Angrist, S. S. 'Role model influences on college women's career aspirations, *Merrill-Palmer Quarterly of Behaviour and Development*, 1971, **17**, 263–79.

Alpert, D. E. 'The struggle for status: accepting the aggressive female executive' *MBA Thesis*, February, 1976, 25–8.

Alvarez, A. and Lutterman, K. G. and Associates *Discrimination in Organization* (Jossey-Bass Inc.: San Francisco, 1979).

Anderson, J. 'Psychological determinants', in *Women and Success* (Kundsen, R., ed.) (Morrow, 1974).

Argyris, C. *Integrating the Individual and the Organisation* (Wiley: New York, 1964).

Ashridge Management College *Employee Potential: issues in the Development of Women* (Institute of Personnel Management, 1980).

Bartol, K. M. 'Expectancy theory, as a predictor of female occupational choice and attitude towards business *Academy of Management Journal*, 1976, **19**, 4, 669–75.

Bass, B. M., Krusell, J. and Alexander, R. A. 'Male managers' attitudes towards working women', in *Women in the Professions: What's all the Fuss About?* (Fidell, L. S. and Delameter, J., eds) Sage Publications: Beverly Hills, London, 1971.

Bond, J. R. and Vinacke, S. 'Coalitions of mixed sex triads, *Sociometry*, 1961, **24**, 61–5.

Bottom Line: (Un)equal Enterprise in America. (1978). The President's Interagency Task Force on Women Business Owners.

Bowman, G. W., Worthy, N. B. and Greyser, S. A. 'Are Women Executives People?' *Harvard Business Review*, 1965, **43**, 14–28, 166–78.

Brown, L. K. 'Women and Business Management', *Signs*, 1979, **5**, (2), 266–88.

Cecil, E. A., Paul, R. J. and Olins, R. A. Perceived importance of selection variables used to evaluate male and female job applicants, *Personnel Psychology*, 1973, **26**, 397–404.

Cleverdon, J. *Women in Management* (The Industrial Society: London, 1980).

Cooper, C. L. 'Coronaries: the risk to working women', *The Times*, (December, 1980).

Cooper, C. L. *Executive Families Under Stress* Prentice-Hall: New Jersey, 1982.

Cooper, C. L. and Davidson, M. J. 'The pressures of working women. What can be done? *Bulletin of British Psychological Society*, 1981.

Day, D. R. and Stogdill, R. M. 'Leadership Behaviour of Male and Female Supervisors; *Personnel Psychology*, 1972, **25**, 353–60.

Dipboye, R. L., Fromkin, H. L. and Wilback, R. L. 'Relative importance of applicant sex, attractiveness and scholastic standing in evaluation of job applicant resumes', *Journal of Applied Psychology*, 1975, **60**, 39–43.

Fenn, M. *Making it in Management: a Behavioural Approach with Women Executives* (Prentice-Hall: New Jersey, 1979).

Fidell, L. S. 'Empirical verification of sex discrimination in hiring practice, *American Psychologist*, 1970, **25**, 1094–8.

Flexman, N. A. *Women of Enterprise: A Study of Success and Failure Incidents from Self-Employed Women Using the Perspectives of Bakan's Constructs of Agency and Communion and Attribution Theory* (Unpublished Doctoral Thesis, University of Illinois, U.S.A., 1980).

Forisha, B. L. 'The inside and the outsider: women in organisations', in *Outsiders on the Inside* (Forisha, B. L. and Goldman, B. H. eds) (Prentice Hall, New Jersey, 1981).

Fox, E. H. 'Business School Survey: Women outpace men in enrolments, *Enterprising Women*, November 1977, **3**, 6.

Fuller, F. and Batchelder, M. 'Opportunities for women at the administrative level,' *Harvard Business Review*, January–February, 1953, 111–28.

Gazzaniga, M. S. *The Bisected Brain*, Neuroscience Series 2 (Appleton-Century-Crofts, 1970).

Gazzaniga, M. S. *The Integrated Mind* (Plenum: New York, 1978).

Goffee, R., Scase, R. and Pollack, M. 'Why some women decide to become

their own bosses', *New Society*, 9 September, 1982, 408–10.
Gutek, B., Nakamura, C. Y. and Nieva, V. F. 'The interdependence of family roles', *Journal of Occupational Behaviour*, 1981, 2, 1, 1–16.
Hampton-Turner, C. *Radical Man* 1981 (Anchor/Doubleday: New York, 1970).
Harlan, A. 'A comparison of careers for male and female MBA's', Working Paper, Wellesley, Mass. (Centre for Research on Women, Wellesley College, 1978).
Hennig, M. and Jardim, A. *The Managerial Woman* (Marion Boyars: London, 1977).
Herbert, T. T. and Yost, E. B. 'Women as effective managers: a strategic model for overcoming the barriers', *Human Resources Management*, 1978, 17, 18–25.
Huffmire, D. 'U.S. business: the sex equality myth', *Industrial Management*, March 1976, 31–2.
Kanter, R. R. *Men and Women of the Corporation* (Basic Books: New York, 1977).
Komives, J. 'Are You One of Them?' *MBA Magazine*, June/July 1973.
Korn Ferry International *Profile of Senior Executives* (Korn Ferry: London, 1982).
Kozoll, C. E. 'The relevant, the honest, the possible: management development for women', *Training and Development Journal*, February 1973, 3–6.
Landau, S. and Bailey, G. *The Landan Strategy* (Seal Books: Toronto, 1980).
Langrish, S. V. *The Training Needs of Women and Men Managers* (EOC/UMIST Conference on Women managers and Postive Action: Manchester, 1983).
Langrish, S. V. and Smith, J. M. *Women in Management: Their Views and Training Needs* (Training Services Division, Manpower Services Commission, 1979).
Langrish, S. V. and Smith, J. M. *Management Development Programme for Women in the Textile Industry* (Manpower Services Commission: London, 1981).
McCaslin, B. S. and McNamara, P. P. *Be Your Own Boss: A Woman's Guide to Planning and Running Her Own Business* (Prentice-Hall: New Jersey, 1980).
McClelland, D. C. *Entrepreneurs are Made, not Born* (Forbes, 1969).
MacDonald, E. 'Women in Management', *British Management Review & Digest*, 1979, 5, 4, 5–8.
Maier, N. R. Male versus female discussion leaders. *Personnel Psychology*, 1970, 23, 455–61.
Megargee, E. I. 'Influence of sex-roles on the manifestation of leadership', *Journal of Applied Psychology*, 1969, 53, 377–82.
Melrose-Woodman, J. 'Profile of the British Manager', *Management Survey Report* No. 38, (BIM, 1978).
Moore, L. M. and Rickel, A. V. 'Characteristics of women in traditional and non-traditional managerial roles', *Personnel Psychology*, 1980, 33, 317–33.

O'Leary, V. E. 'Some attitudinal barriers to occupational aspirations in women', *Psychological Bulletin*, 1974, **81**, 809–28.

Place, H. 'A biographical profile of women in management', *Journal of Occupational Psychology*, 1979, **52**, 267–76.

Pogrebin, L. C. *Getting Yours: How to Make the System Work for the Working Woman*. (Avon Books: New York, 1976).

Robertson, W. 'Women M.B.A's, Harvard, 73', *Fortune*, 28 August 1978, 50–60.

Rosen, B. and Jerdee, T. H. 'Sex stereotypes in the executive suite,' *Harvard Business Review*, March/April, 1974.

Rossi, A. S. 'The working wife: how does she live? What does she want?' *Management Review*, April 1967, 9–13.

Schwartz, E. G. *The Sex Barrier in Business* (Georgia State University Press: Atlanta, 1971).

Sexton, D. L. and Kent, C. A. *Female Executives and Entrepreneurs: a Preliminary Comparison* (Baylor University, U.S.A., 1981).

Shapero, A. 'Have you got what it takes to start your own business?' *SAVVY*, April 1980, 33–6.

Shaw, E. A., 'Differential impact of negative stereotyping in employee selection', *Personnel Psychology*, 1972, **25**, 333–8.

Smith, C. K., Smith, W. S. and Stroup, K. M. (1977). *Counseling Women for non-traditional careers*. Ann Arbour, MI: ERIC Counseling and Personnel Services Information Centre, University of Michigan.

Smith, J. M. *et al*. *Women in Management: A Manual of Training Materials* (Manpower Services Commission: London, 1983).

Smith, K. 'Networking' in *Women in Management: a Manual of Training Materials* (Smith, J. M., ed.) (Manpower Services Commissionn: London, 1983).

Smith, M. J. *When I Say No I Feel Guilty* (Bantam Books, 1975).

Snell, M. W., Glucklich, P. and Povall, M. Equal pay and opportunities', *Research paper No. 20*. (Department of Employment, April 1981).

Staines, G., Tavris, C. and Jayaratne, T. E. 'The queen bee syndrome', *Psychology Today*, January, 1974, 55–60.

Stein, B. A. *Getting there: Patterns in Managerial Success* (Working Paper). (Centre for Research on Women, Wellesley College, Ma., 1976).

Stern, B. B. *Is Networking For You?* (Spectrum Books, 1981).

Terborg, J. R. and Ilgen, D. R. 'A theoretical approach to sex discrimination in traditionally masculine occupations', *Organisational Behaviour and Human Performance*, 1975, **13**, 352–76.

Vogel, S. R., Broverman, I. K., Clarkson, F. E. and Rosenkrantz, P. S. 'Maternal employment and perceptions of sex roles among college students,' *Developmental Psychology*, 1970, **3**, 381–4.

Von Boeschoten, M. 'Men and Women at Work', (*ATM Newsletter* June 1983).

Watkins, J. M. and Watkins, D. S. *The Female Entrepreneur: her Background and Determinants of Business choice – some British data*. (Entrepreneurship Research Conference, Babson College, U.S.A., 1983).

4 Into the second generation of women's training: a sceptic takes stock
Mike Smith

THE ACHIEVEMENTS OF THE FIRST GENERATION

Dating social trends can be a hazardous affair. No sooner has a concensus emerged that a major social development started at such and such a date than somebody identifies an earlier antecedent which relates at least, to the ancient Greeks, or even better, to Cro-Magnon Man and Woman! However, there is probably a stronger than usual concensus that the concern for women's training and development 'took off' almost two decades ago during the late 1960s. The concern culminated in the Equal Pay Act of 1970 and ultimately the Sex Discrimination Act and the foundation of the Equal Opportunities Commission in 1975.

During this time, there has been a veritable flowering of training activities for women. Much of the impetus was provided by the Industrial Training Boards and their training advisers – an influence which continued up to 1982 when most Boards were disbanded. Other organizations have also played their part. Naturally, the Equal Opportunities Commission has encouraged, supported and sponsored a number of initiatives. The Manpower Services Commission has also played a major role in analysing the training need and supporting the development of specific training programmes for women. The MSC has also made a unique contribution in establishing a Women and Training Group consisting of professional trainers who are active in this field. This group aims to encourage the exchange of expertise by means of a programme of training events and a quarterly newsletter.

These, and other developments have resulted in a huge expansion of a type of training for women which is fundamentally different from the traditional women's training in occupational skills such as typing, sewing, assembling. It is hard to classify the new types of training. Some of the training programmes such as the Brooklands program on Wider Opportunities for Women has been concerned with reducing occupational segregation and reducing sex stereotyping of occupations. Other training programmes such as the Brunel University Personal Effectiveness Workshops and the Career and Life Planning Workshops sponsored by the MSC has focussed upon the career problems faced by women such as the short 'promotion ladders' in many of the 'pink collar jobs' and the problems which women may face when they return to work after child-rearing.

Probably the largest type of training for women involve the programmes for women managers such as the programmes developed at Ashridge College, Brunel University and UMIST (Smith *et al.*, 1983). The emphasis on Management Training is fully justified on two grounds: firstly, there are disproportionately few women managers and; secondly, managers often hold the key to decisions concerning others. One way of enhancing the opportunities of women in general is to encourage the promotion of more women into management functions.

Another category of activity also concerns management but it has a different focus. Instead of being concerned with the promotion and prospects of the trainees themselves the focus is upon helping managers and administrators to implement equal opportunity policies within their organizations. An example of this type of activity is the publication by the Manpower Services Commission (1981) of 'No Barriers Here' a guide designed to help organizations develop policies and practices which are fair to both sexes.

Of course, this brief overview of the achievements of the first generation of women's training is incomplete, it merely highlights some of the major trends and it vastly under-represents the larger but less conspicuous activities such as one- or two-hour sessions inserted into general training courses and the establishment of women's networks within organizations. However, even this brief overview is sufficient to demonstrate that the first generation of women's training has had many successes. Indeed, it has been said that the achievements in women's training have 'ballooned' during the last two decades. The metaphor is dangerous because it prompts darker questions. Is the balloon about to burst? Will the EOC go the same way as the ITB's? Will the EOC be merged with some other organization such as the Commission for Racial Equality?

THE DANGER OF DECLINE AND COUNTER-SUGGESTIBILITY

The first generation of training for women undoubtedly shared the rapid, exponential growth which is characteristic of the first phase of many social movements. Unfortunately, many, possibly the majority, of social movements progress to subsequent stages which are less benign. The progression of these stages can be neatly demonstrated by Johnson's (1945) charming and delightful paper, 'The Fantom Anaesthetist of Mattoon'. The paper describes how one inhabitant of Mattoon, a small town in the mid-west of the U.S.A., suffered an attack of hysteria. The victim of the attack attributed her symptoms to a gas which a 'mad prowler' had used. The story received banner headlines from the press and in the following days others reported falling victim to the anaesthetist's attacks. Mattoon organized vigilante patrols to apprehend the mad prowler, but he always managed to avoid being seen or detected.

Gradually, the details of the attacks became preposterous. Expert evidence unanimously declared that no known gas, had properties which were consistent with the reports of the 'victims'. As scepticism grew, victims were sent to hospital for medical and psychiatric observation. Reports of new attacks then rapidly diminished. This delightful incident is unusual because it provides quantitative evidence on the course of a social phenomenon.

Johnson was able to gain access to police records during these eventful days in Mattoon, and he was able to plot the number of calls to the police: the results are shown in Figure 4.1. The graph can be divided into four phases: the baseline phase before the attacks; a phase of rapid expansion; a phase of rapid decline and; a long phase of counter-suggestibility. It is the phases of decline and counter-suggestibility which should concern those with personal investment

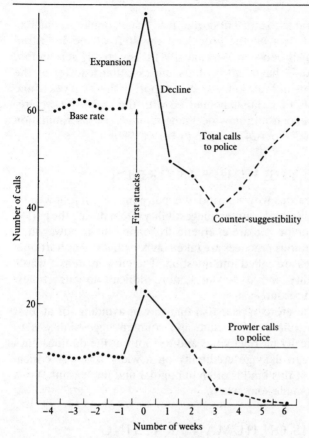

Figure 4.1 The phantom anaesthetist of Mattoon

in training women managers. Unless these phases are avoided the achievements attained in the last generation will be nullified.

Of course, one response to this threat is to deny its existence. It is an easy path since the events in Mattoon seem a far cry from the problems of training women managers. But, the cycle of expansion, decline and counter-suggestibility, so neatly demonstrated by the phantom anaesthetist of Mattoon has a wide generality. It can be seen in other studies in different parts of the world (e.g. The Miracle of Sabana Grande, Tumin and Feldman, 1955; The Phantom Slasher of Taipai, Jacobs, 1958). Perhaps more significantly, the curve almost certainly applies to situations which are more comparable to equal opportunities. For example, if someone had collected data on the growth of the staff of the Industrial Training Boards between 1964 and 1984 it is virtually certain that the graph would have shown the same essential features as the graph of events in Mattoon. A recent report in the *Times* (21 June 1983) suggests that claims connected with the equality laws are, after a large expansion, now declining rapidly: sex discrimination applications fell from 243 in 1976 to 181 in 1980.

PUTTING THE HOUSE IN ORDER

One of the reasons why a period of expansion is often followed by phases of decline and counter-suggestibility is that during the period of boom, when people are energetically joining the bandwagon, a number of dubious practices are taken on board. After a short time these practices are called into question. The movement as a whole loses credibility and it becomes more difficult to attract new members and resources.

It would therefore appear that one way of avoiding, or at least delaying, the phases of decline and counter-suggestibility is to examine critically past activities and to root out the dubious ones before they can damage credibility on a wider scale. A critical examination of this kind is often unpopular and unpleasant. Yet a start must be made somewhere.

EMPHASIS ON HUMAN TRAINING

Perhaps, in the context of management development for women, one of the first areas for examination is the training in social skills. Social skills training comes to the fore simply because it is strongly emphasized in most management development courses for women.

Typically, at least a third of a programme will be devoted to various aspects of dealing with other people such as transactional analysis, assertiveness training, working in groups etc., etc. Unfortunately, all the evidence does not point to such a widespread training need. For instance, many surveys of job satisfaction show that social relationships are one of the most satisfactory aspects of work. When first year students questioned a representative sample of Mancunians using the Job Descriptive Index – a well-established questionnaire produced by Smith *et al.* (1969) the results shown in

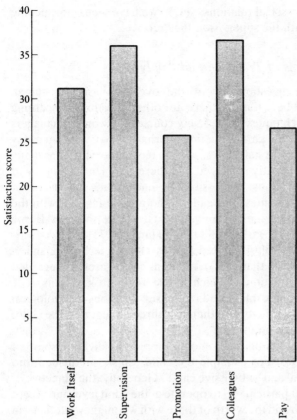

Figure 4.2 Satisfaction of 470 Mancunians with five aspects of their job

Figure 4.2 were obtained. Such high levels of existing satisfaction with co-workers and supervisors seriously weaken claims that there is a widespread need for human relations training.

Scientific analyses of the Managerial Job by Mintzberg (1973) Stewart (1967) and McCall *et al.* (1978) also cast doubt upon such a global need for social skills training. According to these writers the management job is characterized by brevity, variety and fragment-ation. Most interpersonal 'incidents' are of an extremely short duration and managers spend little time with their subordinates. Furthermore, the way that this time is spent will be determined largely by the working situation and the task at hand. Precious little time is spent on social relations, yet, as we have seen, most people are satisfied with the supervision they receive.

Four Criticisms of Transactional Analysis

Even if these questions about the over-emphasis on human relations could be set aside, there are other questions concerning the detailed techniques used. Many courses for women managers devote a substantial part of the time, perhaps two days of a ten-day course, on transactional analysis. It is a technique which has many attractions: it is neatly packaged and there is a plentiful supply of teachers. It is almost impossible to encapsulate transactional analysis into a few lines and readers who are not familiar with the technique should refer to standard texts such as these by Berne (1964, 1972, 1975), Barker (1980) and Harris (1973).

Transactional analysis started as a psychiatric technique and in essence it maintains that human relations can be usefully regarded as a series of transactions in which people trade 'strokes'. This trade in strokes is strongly influenced by the subconscious psychological states of the people involved: there are three basic states, the child, the parent and the adult.

The situation can be made more complex by dividing some of these basic states. For example the child can be subdivided into 'rebellious child' and 'submissive child'. Generally, the objective of training is to get participants to operate at the adult level and accept their own worth and the worth of those with whom they interact – in other words to adopt the life position of 'I'm OK: You're OK'. This description of transactional analysis is too brief to give a totally accurate picture but it gives sufficient information to set into context the four main criticisms of using transactional analysis in the training of women managers.

The first criticism relates to the origin in psychiatric practise. The technique may be a useful tool when dealing with severely disturbed people but this does not mean that it can be generalized, lock, stock and barrel, to settings involving 'normal' people on management training courses. The second criticism centres upon a logical inconsistency. Transactional analysis seeks to encourage others to adopt an 'I'm OK: You're OK' position. Yet perhaps hypocritically, it transmits the underlying message of a parent telling a child that 'you are not OK until you have bought my book, attended my course and have assimilated my way of looking at the world'. The third criticism is on a similar, but slightly different, vein and it is emphatically voiced by Cinnaman and Farson (1979), in their book *Cults and Cons': the exploitation of the emotional growth consumer.* In essence, these critics regard transactional analysis as a fad of the 1960s which has the unfortunate side-effect of exploiting those who are most vulnerable and who are least sure of their own interactions.

Perhaps the most damning criticism of transactional analysis (TA) arises from scientific circles. Many psychologists regard it as a restatement of the old Freudian theory which divides personality into three components: the id, the ego and the superego. Much of Freudian theory has been abandoned by the scientific community because, among other things, no-one has been able to give a convincing demonstration that the human personality is divided into these three parts. The scientific critics assert that the division of 'psychological states' into child, adult and parent is so axiomatic that the transactionists need to offer empirical evidence to support their ideas. The absence of empirical evidence is criticism levelled elsewhere. Even if the theory is accepted, there is scant evidence that the technique can be successfully imparted in an industrial training context. TA may work in the case of intensive, long-term therapy with psychiatric patients. But, those who maintain that a significant change in the behaviour of women managers can be brought about by a one- or two-day course in TA, must provide the sceptics with objective, quantifiable data; subjective reports from the participants or the seminar leaders are not enough.

Assertiveness training and Self-selection

Assertiveness training is another interpersonal skill frequently included in training and development programmes for women. The rationale for its inclusion is very strong. Figure 4.3 gives a schematic representation of the relationship between assertiveness and managerial performance. It suggests that very low levels of assertiveness will achieve little. As assertiveness increases there is a rapid improvement in performance. Then, after an optimum point is reached, assertiveness can turn into aggressiveness, other people are antagonized and effectiveness falls rapidly and quickly.

A number of writers (e.g. Maccoby and Jacklin, 1974; Vaught,

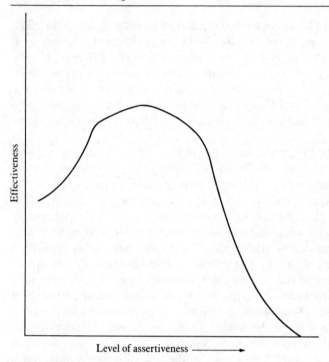

Figure 4.3   Assertiveness and effectiveness

1955; Larwood and Wood, 1977, Schwartz and Waetjen, 1976; and Place, 1979) suggest that women tend to be towards the unassertive end of the continuum. There is clear quantative evidence to support this notion. Probably the best measure of personality is Cattell's 16PF Questionnaire (Cattell, 1956). As, its name implies, the 16PF measures sixteen different facets of personality and one of these facets, factor E, concerns assertiveness. Cattell *et al.* (1970) write that factor E (dominance)

> "tends to be positively correlated . . . with social status and is somewhat higher in established leaders than followers . . . Groups averaging high on E show more effective role interaction and democratic procedure . . . Among occupations, it is most associated with those requiring boldness and courage . . . It is appreciably influenced by heredity and is one of the personality factors distinguishing the sexes".

This conclusion is substantiated by a carefully controlled investigation by Saville (1972) of a sample of 2,217 men and women drawn from the general population. All this data points to an inevitable conclusion: There is a need to train potential women managers in assertiveness.

However, in practice, the inclusion of assertiveness training needs to be undertaken with care. The logic of the previous paragraph applies to women in general. Women on management programs are rarely typical of their sisters. They are often self-selected. It seems that those who volunteer already have a high level of assertiveness. Indeed, there is some empirical evidence to support this notion. As a part of the development process for the UMIST Women in Management Course two sets of participants

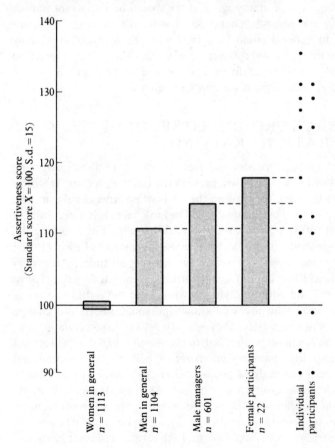

Figure 4.4   **Assertiveness of women participants**

completed the programme which included a module concerned with careers and career planning. On the second day, participants completed a battery of psychological tests designed to provide an objective basis for career plans. The battery of tests included the 16PF Questionnaire and the average assertiveness scores of participants could be calculated. The results are shown in Figure 4.4 Interpretation must be made with care since the two pilot courses at UMIST consisted of a total of 22 participants. However, the implication is that the process of self-selection among volunteers results in a level of assertiveness which is already sufficiently high. Further training in assertiveness could increase levels of assertiveness to the point where it becomes dysfunctional aggression.

If this occurred on any scale, there would be important implications for the second generation of women's training. Women's training in general could be tarred with the brush of producing unreasonable and over-assertive women. The adverse reaction produced in others could well accelerate or even precipitate, a backlash against women's training in general.

THE BACKGROUND TO SECOND-GENERATION TRAINING

Putting the house in order and avoiding the more dubious training activities will not, on its own, prevent the onset of decline. It will be necessary to move forward on the basis of positive developments. While it is easy to use hindsight and to look back, it is more difficult to predict future trends. Prediction can be helped by adopting the three-stage model of the change process suggested by Lewin (1952). The first stage consists of unfreezing existing attitudes. According to Ottaway (1980) the unfreezing process is initiated by the *change generators* – the gifted individuals who select the right issue at the right time and who are well-known personalities. If the change generators are successful they will attract first, *barricade demonstrators*, hell bent on public confrontation, and then they will attract the more polite, *patron demonstrators* who use the formal and conventional channels of power rather than confrontation. Both types of demonstrators arouse the interest of a wide range of people who might benefit from the change and who defend the movement and its aims. When the number of *defenders* become large enough the unfreezing process is complete. In the context of this taxonomy,

attitudes towards women managers have, in many organizations
already been unfrozen. This has been one of the main achievements
of the first generation. Indeed, we now seem to be in the middle of
the second stage of the change process: implementing the change
itself. Again, Ottaway's (1980) classification of change agents is
relevant. The first of the implementors are the *external implementors* – usually freelance consultants engaged in experimental
work. They influence and are superceded by the *headquarters
implementors* employed in either a personnel or organization
development function at the head office of a large company.

The head office implementors in their turn influence the *internal
implementors* before turning their attention to another change they
wish to bring about in their organization. Meanwhile the internal
implementors continue to pursue specific changes at factory-floor
level. When the internal implementors have done their work, the
second of Lewin's stages is complete and a change has been
produced. It would seem that the training of women managers has
almost reached this point: the change generators have made their
reputations and moved on: the barricade demonstrators have
mellowed – a little; and several external consultants are wondering
whether it is time to move to new projects and greener pastures.
Dozens of organizations particularly in nationalized industries, the
service sector and local authorities have nominated someone at
headquarters to be 'responsible' for women's training. In a few
organizations there are internal implementors, drawing up
development programmes for specific women managers, mounting
courses and establishing networks among their women employees.
The activities of the implementors will continue and consolidate
before the final 'refreezing' stage is entered. The transition too from
changing to refreezing can be difficult. Ottaway (1983) writes:

> "Trainees may be training people into a new behaviour which
> should be refrozen but the training does not transfer to the work
> situation where old habits prevail. For change to occur the new
> behaviour has to be adopted and normalized into the day-to-day
> behaviour of the organization this is the task of the . . . adopters.
> The *prototypic adopters* . . . are the first to say 'I'll try it in my
> group' they may be managers, superiors, shop stewards or
> informal leaders. Often change will get this far and fail to refreeze
> and it is the final groups, there who maintain and use the new
> system who are the key to lasting change".

Ottaway's classification is useful because it helps identify the tasks that need to be accomplished by the second generation of women's training. In essence, these tasks are two-fold: to provide residual support for headquarters and internal implementors and, to make it easy for the adopters to refreeze the situation in a new mould.

HELPING THE ADOPTERS

Seen in this light, the question becomes, 'how can the second generation of training help the adopters'. The answer must take account of the fact that in the short- and medium-term, the majority of these adopters will be men. The closer involvement of men will, as Smith (1981) points out, bring the attendant danger of a male backlash. In order to involve men and avoid a backlash it will be necessary to tone down some of the more strident training activities of the initial barricade feminists who may then leave the scene in a display of disgust and anger in response to seeing their ideals 'corrupted'. The trainers who remain will face the problem of how they can influence male adopters.

It seems slightly surprising, therefore, that one of the major tasks in the next generation of *women's* training is to *train men* in how to adopt and adapt to the new situation. It is an essential task since many men act as 'gate-keepers' to the futures of many women. But it will not be an easy one. One of the main difficulties will be overcoming men's resistance to take part in training which concerns women. There appear to be three general approaches. First, there can be *special courses for men*. In practice, these will need to be very short, perhaps lasting only one or one-half of a day and they can be expected to encounter the highest level of resistance. A second approach would be to *slip in sessions* on women in management into more general management courses. For example, it should be possible to include, say, three sessions of two hours each into a week's management course. The third approach should encounter the lowest level of resistance and will consist of *informal contacts*. Unfortunately, the use of informal contacts is very time-consuming and is often very slow. Consequently, it will tend to be used only at the highest management levels.

Although men will form the largest group of adopters an increasing number of the target population will be women. It seems apposite to finish this chapter by considering the training which could help them in their task. There are two particularly important training needs which concern the way that women change adopters relate to other women.

Often we concentrate on the resistance which some men show towards women in management. We are prone to overlook the fact that many women, possibly the majority of women, show similar resistance. Indeed, quite frequently, participants on women's training courses point out that they receive little resistance from men in their organizations. Their difficulties often arise from the reactions of older female subordinates. Training could provide these female adopters with an opportunity to share experiences and develop skills for dealing with this problem.

Finally, we should not overlook a rather different facet of 'women to women' training. A substantial portion of first-generation training concerned the tactics and strategies of promotion. It often emphasized the crucial role which members play in promotion decisions and how mentors can enhance the careers of their protégés. Hopefully, this effort will bear fruit and more women will achieve management jobs in the near future. The possibility then arises of harnessing their power and influence by training them in the skills of being a good mentor to younger subordinates. Indeed, when this situation arises, we will need to start thinking about our objectives for the third generation of women's training.

FURTHER INFORMATION ON TRAINING

For further information on training programmes available for women in management, one could contact the following resource units in the UK:

Training Opportunities for Women. Training Services Division, Manpower Services Commission, Moorfoot, Sheffield.
Women at Work Unit, Department of Management Sciences, U.M.I.S.T., P.O. BOX 88, Manchester.
Equal Opportunities Commission, Overseas House, Quay Street, Manchester.
The Industrial Society, 3 Carlton House Terrace, London SW1.

in the USA:

Women in Management Division, Academy of Management, P.O. Box K2, Mississippi State, Mississippi 39762.

and in Europe:

European Foundation for Management Development, 20 Place Stephanie, 1050 Brussels, Belgium.

REFERENCES

Barker, D. B. *Transactional Analysis and Training* (Gower: Epping, 1980).
Berne, E. *Games People Play* (Penguin: Harmondsworth, 1964).
Berne, E. *What do You Say After You Say Hello* (Corgi Books: London, 1972).
Berne, E. *Transactional Analysis in Psychotherapy* (Condor Books: Souvenir Press, London, 1975).
Cattell, R. B. (1956) *The 16PF* (National Foundation for Educational Research: Windsor, 1956).
Cattell, R. B., Eber, H. W. and Tatsuoka, M. M. *Handbook for the Sixteen Personality Factor Questionnaire* (16PF) (National Foundation for Educational Research: Windsor, 1970).
Cinnaman, K. and Farson, D. *Cults and Cons: the Exploitation of the Emotional Growth Consumer* (Nelson-Hall: Chicago, 1979).
Harris, T. A. *I'm OK – You're OK* (Pan Books: London, 1973).
Jacobs, N. 'The Phantom Slasher of Taipei', *Social Problems*, 1958, 319–29.
Johnson, D. M. 'The phantom anesthetist of Mattoon', *Journal of Abnormal and Social Psychology*, April 1945, 175–86.
Larwood, L. and Wood, M. M. *Women in Management* (D.C. Heath & Co.: Lexington, Massachusetts, 1977).
Lewin, K. *Field Theory in Social Science* (Cartwright, D. ed.) (Tavistock: London, 1952).
McCall, M. W., Morrison, A. and Hannan, R. L. *Studies of Managerial Work: Results and Methods* (Center for Creative Leadership: Greenboro, North Carolina, 1978).
Maccoby, E. E. and Jacklin, C. V. *The Psychology of Sex Differences* (Sanford University Press: California, 1974).
Manpower Services Commission *No Barriers Here* (Manpower Services Commission: Sheffield, 1981).
Mintzberg, H. H. *The Nature of Managerial Work* (Harper & Row: New York, 1973).
Ottaway, R. N. *A Taxonomy of Change Agents*, 3rd edn (Department of Management Sciences: UMIST, Manchester, 1980).
Ottaway, R. N. 'Organizational Change', in *Introducing Organizational Behaviour* (Smith *et al.*, eds) (MacMillan: London, 1983).

Place, H. 'A biographical profile of women in management', *Journal of Occupational Psychology*, 1979, **52**, 267–76.

Saville, P. *British Standardization of the 16PF*, (National Foundation for Educational Research: Windsor, 1972).

Schwartz, E. B. and Waetjen 'Improving the self-concept of women', *Business Quarterly*, 1976, **44**, 4, 20–7.

Smith, J. M. 'Avoiding the Male Backlash', in *Practical Approaches to Women's Career Development* (Cooper, C.L., ed.) (Manpower Services Commission: Sheffield, 1981).

Smith, J. M., Wood, J. E. and Langrish, S. V. *Manual for the UMIST Management Development Programme for Potential Women Managers*, (Gower Press: London, 1983).

Smith, P. C., Kendall, L. M. and Hulin, C. L. *The Measurement of Satisfaction in Work and Retirement: a strategy for the study of attitudes.* (Rand McNally: Chicago, 1969).

Stewart, R. *Managers and Their Jobs* (MacMillan: London, 1967).

Tumin, M. M. and Feldman, A. S. 'The miracle at Sabana Grande', *Public Opinion Quarterly*, 1955, 126–39.

Vaught, G. N. 'The relationship of role identification and ego strength to sex differences in rod and frame test', *Journal of Personality* 1955, **33**, 271–83.

Section 2　Women in Management Jobs

5 Women in television and radio
Olwyn Hocking

INTRODUCTION

At first glance, television and radio seem an industry where women have made rapid advance in recent years. In less than a decade we have moved on from the much heralded arrival of the first regular woman news reader to a time when women presenters seem almost obligatory. That early fuss now seems difficult to comprehend. But is this superficial appearance reflected in the employment patterns of women in the organizations behind the public front? The figures tend to suggest that, in fact, the dispersal of women throughout the career structures in the media are far closer to the patterns found in most large organizations and firms. The news reader on your screen may be a woman – but the person behind the camera is almost certainly a man, while the person who typed the script is almost certainly a woman.

The media differ in one important aspect from many other parts of industry – they have not been as badly affected by the recession. As a result, they are not in the position of companies cutting back staff, where reduced turnover of employees has afforded less opportunity to influence employment patterns. Indeed, radio and television are still growth areas – as shown by the launch of Channel Four, the development of breakfast television and the advent of cable television. The fourth channel has encouraged the growth of smaller independent production units, under the shadow of 18 independent television companies employing nearly 15,000 people, and the BBC providing 29,000 jobs in television and radio. That's not to mention the growing network of independent local radio stations – 38 already with the eventual total expected to be nearly 70.

But the huge diversity of jobs under these general figures makes analysis very difficult. Output varies from drama to documentaries, sport to satellite link-ups. Programme making requires the close co-operation of a vast range of specialist departments such as lighting and sound, wardrobe, props, design – plus all the administrative back-up of accounts, personnel and so on. And the whole industry functions in a context of continual advance in technology, requiring highly trained operators.

The result is a number of posts and responsibilities which are not susceptible to easy categorization. For example, it's not always easy to say which posts fall into the management category, or to answer the question, what is a promotion? Is a news editor management – or a programme producer who happens to be working largely alone? Skills are varied, and the desire to remain involved in the creative field may mean a person could have no wish to be promoted to a better paid more powerful position. It's not possible to automatically assume that women in the middle area of the career structure *want* to rise higher – they could sincerely and for ambitious reasons prefer to stay as producers, for example.

Nevertheless, taking these provisos into account, it does seem possible to draw some clear conclusions from the statistics. The top jobs are held almost totally by men. Further down there is considerable sex segregation – with the areas dominated by women (secretarial and clerical grades) averaging lower pay than those dominated by men (engineering-based grades). Of course, there are many departments where the situation is not so black and white. Studio managers, responsible for operating mixing desks in radio studios, are an example of an area that many women have entered in recent years, and the overall number of women being employed has also risen – although this could be simply reflecting social trends.

However, there is much evidence of an imbalance in employment patterns for men and women. Before asking what managements can do about it, the causes need to be identified. Are they factors within management control – or simply the consequences of earlier influences which lead women to have talents and expectations which are different from those of male employees. Are women staff simply innately less ambitious, by virtue of being equipped for child-bearing? Or is it as some men complain – women simply don't *want* to get on ('You can take a horse to water but you can't make it drink!' was one way of expressing this!)

Many people have strong views on the answers to these questions – but actual research into factors affecting employment patterns for men and women in the media is fairly limited. Most studies seem to have concentrated on women in more clearly defined management roles, in, for example, manufacturing companies, and do not seem strictly applicable to a creative industry with a less hierarchical career structure. The main relevant study was that into Thames Television conducted by Sadie Robarts in conjunction with the Equal Opportunities Commission in 1981. This will be outlined in greater detail in a subsequent chapter, though I shall refer later to its general conclusions.

This raises the first point. It is clear that one of the most useful things a concerned management can do is to undertake its own research to ascertain what is happening to women within its own organization. However, this article in no way sets out to be a piece of research. It is rather an overall description of the industry, concentrating particularly on television, together with reports of the views of different people within it of the reasons for the current employment pattern.

PRESENT DISTRIBUTION OF JOBS

To get an initial impression of the involvement of male and female staff in producing programmes for television, it's interesting to glance at their representation in the credits for a week of television, by checking through the Radio and TV Times. For the BBC, a tenth of the producers were women – 10 compared with 93 men – with three of those producing children's programmes and three in programmes connected with health. Of the directors, seven of the 58 credited were women – again with three in children's programmes. ITV had a higher proportion – a sixth of producers (21 out of 127) and 16 of 111 directors. These figures were boosted by the high proportion of women involved in producing programmes for Channel Four. Eleven of the 21 female producers made Channel

Four items (with another six producing children's programmes), but it should also be remembered that a proportion of Channel Four programmes are contributed by ITV companies.

The overall employment figures drawn up by the BBC show that there are few areas with no women at all – but on the other hand a disproportionate distribution overall. Figures about four years old show women constituting well over a third of all staff, but occupying 82 per cent of all secretarial and clerical jobs compared with 18 per cent of operational staff (technical grades). In between, they held 20 per cent of management and production posts.

A company profile for one of the independent companies tells a similar story. In the engineering, production and craft grades, women held 11 per cent of the jobs, – 131 of 1192 – and nearly half of these were in makeup and wardrobe departments. The rest included 2 camera operators compared with 79 men. A sound department of 83 had no women at all. On an optimistic note, there were more female technical trainees than male. Elsewhere, all 141 secretaries were women, as were all 72 production assistants.

Before going into these categories in more detail, there is one overall factor that is closely bound up in the shortage of women in higher management posts. Most female staff appear to leave between the ages of 25 and 30, whilst male staff have a slower rate of departure – tending towards a higher average length of service. Since it is usual to be older than 30 to have acquired adequate experience for promotions, there are clearly fewer women than men with suitable experience to merit such jobs.

CAREER BREAKS

So why do women leave in such droves? The most obvious argument would seem to be that women are leaving to have children – though to explain the figures, that would require that these women decide to leave permanently. A second suggestion is that women find their careers reach a cul-de-sac. By their late twenties they reach the conclusion they are unlikely to progress and leave to try elsewhere. A complication is that these two factors could be interconnected. Boredom and disappointment with work could contribute to a decision to opt instead for motherhood and family.

Assuming those in the first school of thought to be correct, we must then ask why these employees decide *not* to return to the same place of work. With about 50 per cent of the female population now working, it is clear that many women do not withdraw permanently from the labour force. Many are simply choosing not to return to the same organization.

What could managements do to encourage this return? – especially as the present situation represents a continual drain of the investment of training and experience of female staff. One cited reason for not returning at once was that the seven months' statutory maternity leave was simply not long enough. It forced a very difficult choice on women who wanted more time with a baby. Britain has a very ungenerous maternity provision compared with other Common Market countries, and few companies have allowed very much more than the leave permitted by law.

Various means to make the return to work easier for the mother of a young child have been experimented with. Creche facilities at the place of work were once a priority request by women trying to promote equal opportunities, and are still the subject of campaigns in a number of companies. An experiment by the BBC at Birmingham was tried for about seven months but was said to have too little use to justify the expense. By April 1975 there were four children there full-time and four part-time – including children of people who didn't work for the BBC. The closure did lead to some criticism that the experiment was not tried for long enough. Long term demand is difficult to judge – there is the argument that women will only adjust their plans for families and careers once a creche is well-established – and these things take time! But there is also evidence that some women would prefer child care near the home rather than work. This avoids having to take the baby to work every day, and also helps to avoid distraction while at work. Under the Thames Television scheme, financial help is provided towards outside child care, rather than providing a creche on the premises.

More flexibility in arranging hours of work and the number of hours worked is the other main way to assist with the return to work, either through job sharing or allowing part-time work for a period of time. The long hours that television and radio broadcast means that categories of work exist where a number of people can carry out the same functions and do so in shifts – and there can be more possibilities for job sharing or part-time work in these areas than perhaps the 9 to 5 office where a presence is required throughout set hours by one person with set responsibilities.

The policy of the BBC was outlined by Mr Roger Johnson, Controller of the Appointments whose brief includes supervision of the corporation's equal opportunities policy. He said that there was a very small amount of job sharing, and that part-time work for women returning from maternity leave was considered, where feasible. However, he did feel that there were some areas where the nature of the industry precluded part-time work. Strenuous production schedules, often combined with unpredictable working times, were unavoidable – and could not be structured to cope with someone who could only work a certain number of hours. He felt production teams themselves would quickly resent anyone unable to offer total commitment at the times required.

This was a sentiment also expressed by some women who felt that some jobs were so demanding that they could not be combined with even a small amount of commitment to family life – even with some assistance from management. The other main argument against reduced hours was that this was of little help for women on lower earnings or who were the sole earners.

A final view on the reason why some women don't return to work after maternity leave was that a number feel guilty about causing a 'nuisance' to their employers by keeping their job open, so that temporary staff are required to fill the post. In fact a temporary opening can prove a useful tool in helping to give other staff training and experience – and a number of companies already have a system of 'attachments' whereby people formally take up another job for a limited period, before returning to their own post. It was felt that personnel departments could have a firmer policy to make it quite clear that women do have a right to keep their jobs open.

Turning now to the other suggested factor for the departure of female staff – lack of career prospects as an incentive for staying at work. One general argument that can be put here is that the media is not like a business firm with a clear ranked structure of responsibility and reward. In the media, men too face an unclear career pattern, with disappointments and dead ends.

Women I spoke to tended to agree that open anti-female bias was not a great problem. But there was a complaint shared by women on lower grades that they were not regarded as people with potential. They felt there was a general assumption that they were happy to stay where they were – which was not true!

From the employment statistics quoted earlier, it is obvious that most women are recruited at secretarial level. One route of advancement could be within the 'service' departments such as accounts or personnel which are tending to promote more women. The other usual way would be to transfer to secretarial posts in production offices. From there the grades go up through becoming a transmission assistant (aiding the director) to becoming a production assistant (PA) helping the producer of a programme throughout, such as by organizing film schedules, costing, and studio recordings. Up to that level the posts are held almost exclusively by women. From there, some women go on to become vision mixers – operating studio gallery desks under the guidance of the director. But on the whole, the career path gives the impression of being like a narrowing funnel.

Obviously, there are only a limited number of posts and promotions – and many men as well as women will be disappointed. But there is still some feeling that a whole section of possible recruits have less of a chance of following a career path – the section where most of the women are to be found.

It's interesting to compare these prospects for Production Assistants with those for a roughly equivalent grade which has traditionally attracted more male recruits, that of station assistants in television. They are responsible for a wide range of duties, including managing the studio floor, preparing graphics and gathering materials for studio demonstrations. There is an accepted route of progression to becoming directors – and one of the reasons that more women are becoming directors is because they have realized this and switched from secretarial departments to becoming station assistants.

In the cases of the production assistant and the station assistant, both are very familiar with studio recording, filming on location, and many of the elements going into a programme. But in both cases the jump to the next stage in the career progression involves additional skills to those displayed in the previous job. Success depends on being given a chance to try out the extra elements, and this could obviously be affected by whether a manager feels a person has potential. If he or she considers a person has no potential then this viewpoint could prove self-fulfilling. Generally, it could prove helpful to examine how career paths tend to work in an organization, to see why some lead on while others do not.

But it could still be argued that if women really want to get on, they should never enter at a level where all the evidence suggests they are going to get trapped. They are still believing the old adage of 'getting into telly' by the back door. Here, it is difficult to ignore the influences of the wider world. Many women do leave school with few aspirations and little confidence in their ability. Many will have tended to acquire secretarial qualifications without thinking too deeply about their futures. But once they have settled into a job, some do find that they are on top of their work. Only at that stage does the realization dawn that they could achieve more. It is at that point that the approach of management could make a great deal of difference, either through offering opportunities to try out other jobs or providing 'remedial training.' By doing so, it could help to reduce the imbalance in the workforce employment pattern, and also take advantage of latent skill in its staff.

RECRUITMENT PRACTISES

Now let's move on from the subject of how women can escape from a 'ghetto' to how they can break in to the areas traditionally dominated by men. These are the more technical jobs, which abound in the media, particularly television. Some recent BBC figures show that of the women employed in engineering departments, the biggest single group by far were administrative assistants (72), followed by drawing office personnel (53). The main area of breakthrough in terms of operating equipment is in local radio where a number of women occupy the post of studio manager (known in local radio as station assistants).

For jobs requiring science qualifications, the great shortage of suitably qualified women has obviously been the major factor. Nowadays there are increasing efforts in schools to encourage girls to take science subjects, and the media can play its part in changing attitudes, such as by ensuring literature for careers departments does not always show men behind the controls. Recent advertisements showing women behind cameras do seem to show that this point is appreciated.

However, not all recruitment is at a level where the disparity in qualifications need have an impact. The level at which many trainees enter is one where few paper qualifications are required. The minimum is usually a number of O levels including maths and physics O levels. The research conducted for the Thames Television scheme suggested that that was not strictly necessary, and so tended to operate as a form of indirect discrimination. It acted to deter female candidates, yet was not vital for a successful candidate.

One woman training to be an engineer pointed out another element of the recruitment procedure which is understandable but could have the effect of keeping out women. The sheer weight of applications at trainee level means that interviewers devise extra requirements simply to sift the numbers down. This means that in addition to the examinations needed, candidates tend to be questioned closely about technical matters such as the technical details of how cassette tapes record. At the age of 18, many girls will not have come across these matters, although boys will tend to have picked up information in group discussions or been shown by fathers or uncles. The fact a girl might have less knowledge about cassettes need not reflect less aptitude for technical matters but simply a different background.

Indeed, the woman making this point, who was taken on with an electronics engineering degree, said she is sure she would *not* have been accepted if she had applied at 18. Although she had Maths and Physics A levels, she had little practical experience. She felt lack of such experience would not detract from the ability of a trainee to learn – the basics are all dealt with as part of the training.

Her conclusion was that interview panels should examine carefully what extra requirements they bring in as a device for making selections. Otherwise they could unintentionally reject female candidates who could be quite capable of filling the post. Reviews of this kind will obviously not totally transform the situation – but would seem to be necessary if inroads are to be made into the present all-male domain.

EXTERNAL CONDITIONS

It seems impossible to account for the decisions women make about their careers, and their job performance, without considering the effects of wider social factors. Many women considered that present conditions make it inevitable that women will tend to bear more domestic responsibilities. Women tended to feel they had too many commitments – that professional and social expectations pulled them in different directions.

There was especially a complaint that women have to try extra hard to prevent domestic circumstances affecting work. Some women would give any reason for arriving late or leaving early rather than admit it was because of a child's illness. They felt they would be blamed for it and that their 'image' of coping with work and children would suffer. Yet they felt there was an opposite interpretation for men facing a domestic crisis. They would openly take time off, perhaps to collect children from school, if their mother was ill, and even win sympathy or praise from colleagues of the 'isn't he marvellous' kind. Thus, there was a feeling that not only do women have to bear more of the burden of domestic duties, they have to do so in the context of a less accommodating attitude at work. It's an extra strain that might tip the balance and persuade some women that it's easier to give up work instead.

The conflict between work and family is obviously common to women in many workplaces. On the plus side, as far as the media is concerned, it seems fairly free of the kind of restrictive 'old boy' networks that exist in some types of company, such as that summed up in the image of settling business on the golf course. Traditions such as that obviously make it difficult for women to break in and prove themselves as successful as male colleagues.

THE FUTURE

So what attempts have been made to change the present imbalance? A number of employers are committed to statements declaring a policy of equal opportunity, but the first company to implement a programme of positive action was Thames Television. This followed a long research project which made clear the imbalance within the organization and the dissatisfaction of many women with that situation. The programme included the appointment of an Equality Officer with fulltime responsibility for implementing the policy, backed by an action committee drawn from all levels of staff. Monitoring was to be carried out, looking particularly at applications for jobs, appointments and promotions. Training of staff was to be encouraged, both by making sure people were aware of opportunities, and through devising training courses for management to increase their awareness of the equal opportunities policy. Child care assistance was to be extended.

A first impression is that it has certainly made an impact. One of the first special training weekends for women was set up in conjunction with other companies, with just 6 places available for Thames Television staff. The organizers discovered they had opened a floodgate of enthusiasm – more than 150 applied! The number of women managers has already increased, and a booklet for management training been produced.

The BBC is also a declared equal opportunity employer, having introduced a 'promulgation' ten years ago. It has monitored the overall employment of women, backed up by a certain amount of research including a survey of women taking maternity leave. One area showing marked change is the recruitment of graduate trainees. Last year the number of women news trainees outstripped that of men – from original applications by 496 women and 529 men there were 4 men and 8 women appointed. Women also benefitted from arranged attachments. Attachments were mentioned earlier as a means by which BBC employees gain extra experience. These are decided either by competition or arranged specifically for an individual. Of this latter kind, 45 per cent were for women – a higher percentage than that of women in the workforce. But women have not fared as well in competitive attachments. When it comes to the training of people who will sit on interview boards, the need to be aware of the equal opportunity policy is included in training courses. But not all people who sit on boards undergo such training – so that the training is not comprehensive. The major difficulty for the policy would appear to be its visibility. For example, the willingness to consider part-time work for women returning from maternity leave does not seem to be generally known.

The major unions with membership in the media have policies committing them to promote equal opportunity. The Association of Cinematography Television & Allied Technicians (ACTT) has appointed an equality officer to promote the causes both of women members and those belonging to ethnic minorities.

In conclusion, then, it would appear that prospects for women in radio and television have improved, in line with general trends in society and growing awareness about the issue of equal opportunity for women. There seem grounds for expecting this trend to continue, as personnel departments incorporate equal opportunity statements into the actual practices of management. Nevertheless, the overall figures remain imbalanced – and it suggests that greater investigation of the way organizations actually function would be needed to have a greater impact on the present situation.

REFERENCES

The figures included in this chapter have been obtained from the following sources.
IBA–TV and Radio Handbook, 1983
BBC Digest of Statistics, 1982
Account of the Thames Positive Action Project, 1980–1
Sadie Robarts, Project Officer
Figures at 16 December, 1979
Thames Television – a company profile, 1983
Incomes Data Service
BBC, 1982, Trainee Schemes (non-engineering)

6 Women in marketing and the service industries
Hester A. Thomas

'Marketing is a marvellous job for a woman,' said a Marketing Manager who at the age of twenty-six was working for a multinational company, having previously worked in marketing for Beecham and Unilever. When I asked her to explain, she replied, 'Because it has a freelance quality to it, in that you can move from company to company quite easily. And it pays well.'

The trades of marketing and selling are as old as each other. Before a successful sale can be made, a 'desirable' good has to be found and offered to a suitable person or market. However, whilst the principles of marketing have been the same since time immemorial, the actual profession is a recent one. It has quickly built itself into an industry supported and maintained by a series of service industries such as advertising, market research, postal sales, design and packaging groups, and business consultancies. It has developed its own management hierarchy, from Assistant Brand Manager to the glory of Group Marketing Director, who may represent that group at main board level. The possibilities for the growth of the marketing industry are as wide as the number of products on or being developed for the market.

Marketing became a recognized profession in the late 1950s as some progressive companies saw that markets were becoming more competitive with the rapid development of products, competitors home and abroad, communications and technology, elements which were often outside the influence of the individual company but to which they could and must respond if they were to remain in profitable business. These forward-looking companies invested money in individuals whose task it was to ensure that goods were currently sold to the correct market at the right price and that suitable goods would be developed and marketed for the future. The function of marketing therefore became integral to the development of a given business.

As such, marketing is a stimulating, pressurized and stressful occupation demanding an ability to understand and react quickly to situations with a never-ending supply of energy. The hours are frequently long and unsociable, covering evenings and sometimes weekends. Longer periods of time are spent away from home when travelling both nationally and internationally.

Considering these last points I was surprised to hear marketing being described as a marvellous job for a woman, when so many women's careers are curtailed by the demands of their personal life which so often requires them to be at home, or at least, near at hand. However, if that consideration could be temporarily pushed aside and a career in marketing could be assessed, there are some points which might attract a new single independent recruit, especially if the recruit was female.

As a new profession, it is new to both men and women. It has none of the precedents or traditions which are indelibly a part of the male-dominated professions such as banking, medicine and law. The cultural and sexual discrimination with which these professions are inbued is exhausting and exacerbating for any woman who is not one of the male 'norm'. Marketing does not have such a history. If it should develop it would be a sign of atrophy in a profession whose integrity depends on its ability to reflect current times and contend with the future, rather than dabble in a self-congratulatory manner with a redundant past.

There *are* some women in marketing and the service industries which surround it. Therefore contact *can* be made with other women which may prevent a feeling of isolation – a feeling which assaults many women who accept a job only to find that they are the first woman to be 'trialled' in such a post. This contact, even on a fleeting basis, does offer a means of support, inspiration and information.

For the woman who is keen to follow a career *within* marketing, she will be expected to change jobs both within and without the

Company, seeking opportunities to develop her ability and skills. As such, her long-term career development lies primarily in her hands. Marketing is basically a meritocracy and it is generally true that those who are good will succeed in gaining a place within another company. At a time when the job market is contracting and when the greatest aim for many people is to maintain their present job, such movement is extra-ordinary. It imbues the individual with confidence not only in themselves, but in their power to affect their career to their advantage. This is particularly significant for the woman who, all too often is familiar with the constraints which employers and colleagues can place on her career by *their* attitudes and behaviour. The apparent flexibility of a marketing career may be used by some women to their advantage, planning their job moves to coincide with the development of their personal life.

For the woman who wants to develop her career into other business areas, marketing is an excellent place to start. As marketing lies at the hub of business, marketing managers come in contact with all the surrounding services, so gaining an insight and knowledge of their functions. She will also be a highly visible member of a key department.

On a practical level, it *could* be said that women have as much, if not more knowledge, about the general market-place. Women purchase 80 per cent of consumer goods and have a familiarity with the market, as consumers. Also, the new marketing manager is part of a rising group of relatively affluent women. Women's earnings are increasing relative to men's earnings – in 1970 women's earnings amounted to only 63 per cent of men's earnings; by 1981 this figure had risen to 75 per cent. Their spending power and influence will increase to spread into other markets, such as the financial markets, where the major growth area is that presented by women. She may then be working for a market of which she is part. This empathy with the market is important to any marketing manager for unless there is some basic familiarity with products and the reasons for consumer choice, it is unlikely that the individual will have the knowledge needed to develop and position a product.

A further help in positioning a product for the right age and social group, with a 'message' that they will understand, is to have an understanding of current social trends, attitudes and behaviour. Many of the current social changes are being instigated by women and are affecting their lives. Judie Lannon, Research Director for J. Walter Thompson, explained that her research shows that women's roles are changing. 'Women do not have a rigid view of themselves. They see themselves as multi- rather than single-roled.' This self-perception on the part of women is in direct conflict with the popular images of women which advertisers so often use to complement their product. An increase in the number of women working in marketing should bring some fresh thinking into the profession and help combat the current cliched portraits of women which appear in advertising.

Finally, whilst marketing is an extremely stressful job, demanding a commitment in terms of long hours and prolonged concentration, it *does* provide the type of income which helps to cope with a disrupted home-life.

So there are, apparently, many reasons to substantiate the claim that 'Marketing is a marvellous job for a woman.' But if this really *is* so, why are there not more women working in it? Why is it that the majority of women are below the age of thirty and the majority of men are any age? Why is it that virtually all the junior positions are held by women and all the senior positions by men?

In order to answer these questions it is necessary to return to the issue which was earlier pushed aside: that of the conflict for a woman between her career and personal life. For whilst it may be possible for a new female recruit to assess her immediate future with regard only to herself (as is equally true for a man in that position) it is impossible for a married woman who may also be responsible for children as well as her husband. For her the pressures of doing a good job at both work and home can affect her career potential.

Judie Lannon regards *her* success as exceptional. Despite market research being viewed as a 'woman's area' she was one of the first women to accept a senior market research position in a U.K. advertising agency and is well aware of the difficulties which women face in developing their career and personal life. In her opinion there are few women in top jobs because 'most women find two careers too much for them.'

Tina Hancock started work as a secretary. She is now director of Condor Public Relations, and got there with 'hard graft and no magic.' Like most people she works long, erratic hours and sees herself 'juggling' to cope with her two careers at work and home. 'Women inevitably have the ultimate responsibility, particularly if you have a child'. Even though she has a nanny to help look after her baby she is still 'the one who does all the planning'.

Anne Ferguson, who is a marketing manager, believes that most women realise the dilemma between work and personal life and says that women must decide which are the priorities in their lives and then follow them. 'I decided to work *and* be married', she said.

Another woman who started out as a secretary and rose to be director of Welbeck Public Relations, is Anne Wright. She summed up the differences between men's and women's experience of their work-life: 'We don't have wives to go home to'.

Yet, despite this they are still expected to fulfil all the duties that a wife at home would do as well as continue a full-time job. No matter how understanding or supportive the husband, he still expects his wife to manage the house and himself. Tina Hancock, not without irony, commented, 'A man worries whether he will be late home for his dinner. A woman worries, whether she will be late home to make the dinner.'

However, with a support team of cleaner and nanny, all this can just about be coped with. The real test comes when a woman decides whether or not to have children. The question usually becomes a crucial one when she is entering her thirties. On the one hand a woman feels that time is pressing, on the other she has probably gained a good foundation for her career and may be in a position where she can afford to employ a nanny. But the ultimate success of her career is not secured and she may find the pressures of being both a wonderful mother and a still promising employee just too much. Despite her 'juggling' Tina Hancock still sometimes feels 'guilty in areas'. Judie Lannon sees this guilt as 'crippling' and believes that the 'demands of a domestic life pose an insuperable problem for women,' and one which, until it is resolved, will prevent too many women reaching management levels.

'Where are all the women over thirty?' asked one woman, herself over thirty with three children, a husband, nanny, home and career as creative director, to manage. She was taking a further degree at night school to ensure that come what may she would be suitably qualified for some kind of job in the future.

As for some of the 'other women' presumably they had 'chosen' to stay at home with their children and without the nanny. But what kind of choice is this when the odds are 'insuperable' and so heavily weighted against any woman having the energy to cope with all these demands? And why is it that men do not face the same choice? Yet, legislation for equal opportunities has gone a long way in opening doors for some women. Since 1976, when a leading multinational chemical company issued an Equal Opportunity Policy Statement, it has actively recruited and offered jobs to women graduates and commercial trainees. Of those women, several are employed in marketing functions.

Sue Young entered the company in 1976 at the age of eighteen, as a commercial trainee. She is now a full-time marketing officer. 'Women graduates and someone like myself are probably treated as well as the men at our level. As a group, we're encouraged more positively than the majority of women who are still doing lower-grade clerical type jobs. No-one has raised their expectation or mobility.'

Tamsayne Beesley has been with the company for almost three years, has progressed from sales into marketing and has recently returned from a short secondment to Austria. She is pleased with the way her career has developed to date, especially since she gained a manager who she feels will give her career good guidance. Yet, despite this, she believes that the company 'hasn't yet grappled with what it means to employ women who want careers.' Whilst the company has offered them equal terms of employment, the treatment for women is not always the same as it is for men. 'There's the feeling with some people that women are playing around with careers and sooner or later they'll settle down and have babies or follow their husband.' When this opinion and lack of confidence in women emanates from top management (who are men) it is reasonable to deduce that a woman will have to be better than her male colleagues to succeed in the long term.

The concept of equality of opportunity becomes a myth when it is administered by people whose attitudes are inherently discriminatory. Jan Hall has been in marketing for four years, moving from consumer to industrial marketing. Through her many job moves she has gained enormous experience and is keen to see her career develop long-term within marketing. She believes that the problem of being a woman, rather than a person, may emerge as one becomes more senior in rank and age. 'Many of the men here are aware that they shouldn't be anti-women but they're governed by long-standing, in-built prejudices. When challenged they can't justify their views.'

Much discrimination against women is indirect and, in a single instance, can be exceedingly petty – so petty that nothing is ever done about it. Repeated, and it can become irritating in the extreme. Sue Young feels that much indirect discrimination comes in throwaway remarks, 'usually related to being a woman, your role, or your appearance. It's a way of belittling women which is especially pernicious in a business situation where it distracts from the main subject'. As most women believe that a formal complaint on these situations would be dismissed as not being serious enough to merit attention, the only option for a woman is to explain to a man why she finds his words or actions offensive. As Tamsayne Beesley said, 'You just don't have the energy to cope with that all the time.' Whilst this may be a new professional area for both sexes and although women may be able to set precedents more easily than in other areas, they are *still* confronting men's stereotyped expectations of them.

These expectations often appear as criticisms referring not just to how a job is performed, but *how* it is performed considering it is done by a woman. A certain amount of resilience to such criticism has to be built up. 'It's difficult to realize how much women take in their stride without thinking twice,' said Jan Hall. 'Often we ourselves don't recognize the additional pressures until we sit down and talk about them.'

Other pressures emerge for a woman when she finds that there is not the same distinction between work and home as there is for a man. For her the two are inextricably linked. Shopping lists are made in taxis on the way to the airport, plans are made well in advance for meals and for who will take care of the children. Even the unexpected is coped with. One woman told how she received an urgent telephone call during a meeting. It was her secretary passing on a message from her husband to say that he had invited his managing director home to dinner that evening. During lunch she politely excused herself and rushed out to buy food for the meal, accepting without anger or complaint that it was her husband's privilege and her duty to cater (literally) for such occasions. Women cope in ways a man is never required to do. Whereas he may be good at one thing, she must be good at them all.

Nicki Webster, head of television production at Foote, Cone and Belding, believes that because women's lives are based on practicalities this makes them down to earth and able to make decisions more quickly than men. 'Working together with women, you get the job done.' This view was shared by Anne Ferguson who described women as being 'a jolly sight quicker at the logical process' and 'braver in their decisions.' Tina Hancock felt that because women generally had a broader experience than men they were able to bring more to a job.

Women's social training, which requires them to be good and sympathetic listeners who react to what they hear means that, according to Judie Lannon, as well as 'quickly recognizing the nature of the job and getting on with it,' women are more sensitive to criticism and will adapt and gain from it. 'Women change through a job more than men.' Women are not only coping but are positively grappling with those aspects which could work against them and turning them to their advantage.

Women have been successful and doubtless will continue to be so. As more women are seen in senior positions so their presence will become more familiar and acceptable. As Tina Hancock put it, 'the more men are exposed to women executives, the better it will be for us'. But if getting there remains as tough as it presently is, then there will still be far fewer women than men. Tamsayne Beesley felt that, 'There haven't been enough women before me to make it any easier. Perhaps in twenty years time . . .' Sue Young was a little more optimistic: 'We'll be more successful than previous generations of women but I'm still not sure just how *many* women will survive in management'.

So what does the future hold for women? Companies may be recruiting women in greater numbers but unless they realize the need to help women to stay, they will lose many of them. Women are often viewed, erroneously, as short-term prospects. In a country where 57 per cent of women between the age of 20 and 54 work, 'more men leave for other jobs than women to have babies,' according to Edwina Murrills, senior marketing executive for Anglia Marketing, who added: 'Women are more loyal to a firm.'

If women are to be given careers which make unusual demands on their time and energy and which at some point may conflict with their personal life, then it seems sensible for a company to continue its investment in this person by encouraging her to stay, with the offer of extended maternity (or for her husband, paternity) leave, the facility of flexible hours for a period of time or the facility of a creche. 'Women especially need help when they have babies,' remarked Anne Ferguson. 'The State won't help them so companies must.'

Some companies *are* offering individual women help. Welbeck Public Relations allowed Anne Wright to work part-time after the birth of her second child. Whilst it is laudable that there may be some flexibility shown to individuals within companies, it is little consolation to the remaining women who may not be offered such a liberal approach to maternity leave. What *is* needed is an authorized maternity scheme which will help *all* women.

Legislation for equal opportunities has little real meaning whilst the tasks of looking after the home and caring for children remain those of one sex alone. 'Men still expect women with children to stay at home with them,' said one marketing manager who felt that many men had sympathy with the child's presumed happiness and no interest in the mothers'. There is a need to educate men to consider women as people with their own rights on all issues. It is also important that men look to what they may gain in the form of a less rigid work life, one which is integrated with caring for their family, a caring which extends beyond the purely economic and in which their wives are seen as having the right to a larger life than that defined by the confines of the home and the unpaid drudgery of repetitive work within it.

There *are* certain qualities needed to have a career in marketing, not least of which are mental acuity, creativity and initiative –talents which both men and women possess. But careers, by their very nature are exclusive. Women have been and to some extent are still excluded from them – because they are women. 'Why should women work twice as hard as men to get accepted or promoted?' asked Sue Young, who highlighted the different standards which are used to assess the two sexes. Tamsayne Beesley believes that men feel threatened by women and see them as unfair competition. But Jan Hall considered that a man's feeling of being under threat was a reasonable response to a realistic situation. Marketing is still a less obvious choice for many women, so the women who do apply have often made a carefully thought-out decision and are therefore highly committed. Whilst women do generally tend to lack confidence in their ability to succeed, and it is this self-uncertainty which can cause them to limit themselves, those women who do present themselves for interview are usually more confident than their peers. From this self-selected group of exceptional women, employers choose the best. 'I naturally don't kow-tow to others, but I recognize that this is not typical of all women,' said Jan Hall. 'At the moment, women *do* have to be very confident to succeed and this means that a lot of ordinary women are excluded where ordinary men would cope.' As soon as these women work within a company, they soon stand out. Jan Hall: 'The few women here are bright and ambitious, reflecting the imbalance in recruitment. It *can* be intimidating to some men.' What *is* needed is for management to show a level approach to recruitment and promotion on the basis of the ability of its employees as people, not women and men.

At the same time there is a need for more women to present themselves with the qualities of assertiveness and confidence. 'Women need their confidence boosted,' said Patricia Mann Director at J. Walter Thompson. 'There is a tendency for women to wait for careers to arrive when in fact you have to make them happen.'

If overt discrimination is ever shown towards a woman, there is a formal system for complaint within a company. Few companies offer any comparable system to deal with covert discrimination. This latter type of discrimination is consistently used verbally and physically to cause harrassment to women. There is a need to enlighten the *whole* workforce, male and female, over what constitutes discrimination, that it happens not only at the level of who gets what job, but that it is also apparent in attitudes and assumptions about what women *should* be, rather than the assumption that a woman can be whatever she wants to be. Only when the subject is taken seriously and when management also talk openly and honestly about their concerns and the reticence they feel towards the planning and promotion of women in long-term careers will they be able to take positive actions to support women.

The development of women managers will be a gradual process but it *is* happening and it will continue to happen. It will progress more quickly if companies are prepared to accept the challenge of providing equal *opportunities* rather than equal treatment of women and men. It is not surprising that the most that many companies have done since the Equal Opportunity and Sex Discrimination Acts were passed, is only to include an equal opportunity statement on their job advertisements and to pay lip-service to the meaning of this statement. For the *meaning* of equal opportunities has evolved since the Acts were passed and it is only when the meaning is *understood* that the need *positively* to develop women managers will be perceived.

Until this is realized, there will remain some truth in the statement that 'marketing is a marvellous job for a woman.' But that truth will be uneasy and will allow women to have careers so long as they can squeeze themselves into a pre-formed mould. That mould will require them to be young, single and exceptionally good. That they are exceptionally good will not necessarily be a guarantee that their career will continue to progress in their thirties or if they are married with children. It also indicates that other professions are less good for women (than men) and highlights the issue that most professions do not provide for female employees. Whilst substantiating the claim it is possible to find some points which are especially pertinent for women – but they are *all* also equally true for men. *Where* then is the advantage for being a woman in marketing?

As long as a statement that 'Marketing is a marvellous job for a woman' is tolerated, it pushes women into a ghetto which is not part of the mainstream area of work and which supports the status quo. This will *not* help develop woman as managers although a few may slip through, as they have slipped through in the past – against the odds.

Only when all the issues which face women are confronted – the exhausting demands of practically supporting a home, partner, the caring of children and resisting the worry that you may not have given your best to them all – will women be given the chance to develop to their full potential. *Then* marketing will become a marvellous job for everyone.

Section 3 Implementing Equal Opportunities and Career Development for Women Managers

7 Preparing a positive action programme in an organization
Elizabeth Ball

EQUAL OPPORTUNITY

Equal opportunity in employment is a policy to ensure that all personnel activities will be designed and conducted so that each individual's chance of employment and promotion and their pay should not be affected by her or his sex, marital status, race ethnicity, age or disability. It gives individuals the chance to compete with others and not be denied fair appraisal, or be excluded by the operation of employment policies and practices or attitudes. Essentially, it is the operation of recruitment and promotion by merit and the operation of a pay and benefits policy based on equal reward for equal skill.

WHAT IS DISCRIMINATION?

In the 1970s, the Race Relations, Sex Discrimination and Equal Pay Acts were passed with the intention of making discrimination unlawful in employment, education and the provision of services. Discrimination was thought to be easy to define and recognize, as it was thought to be a phenomenon found chiefly in the bigoted statements of individual and written rules and instructions. It is now clear that discrimination operates in a number of subtle ways. Many discriminatory practices are not intentional, are not perceived to be discriminatory and may occur without anyone directly observing them.

Direct Discrimination

Direct Discrimination, as defined by the Sex Discrimination and Race Relations Acts, is any action which specifically excludes a person or group of people from a benefit or opportunity because a personal characteristic such as sex or ethnicity is applied as a barrier. It is unlawful.

The 'women can't' or 'we do not want women here' syndrome is an obvious and clear example of direct discrimination. But direct discrimination is not always intentional and visible. Many people discriminate by unconsciously applying stereotypes to individuals or by assuming racism or sexism in other people. Thus, a person may reach a decision which is directly discriminatory in effect, which she or he feels is based on a rational decision.

For example, an interviewer interviewing for trainee managers may feel that a woman in her late twenties might prove a less reliable employee because she is likely to have children and take maternity leave. Also the interviewer may feel that a largely male work force would not take well to being managed by a woman. Such feelings would clearly disadvantage women in competing with male candidates. Although the train of thought is directly discriminatory in effect, because it is based on unexamined stereotypes, the interviewer has not expressed the obvious prejudice that women cannot be managers.

Indirect Discrimination

Indirect discrimination is defined by the Sex Discrimination and Race Relations Act as a condition or requirement, which is not job-related and, therefore is not justifiable, with which it is more difficult for women or minority ethnic people to comply and is detrimental to their opportunities. This is indirect discrimination by unreasonable requirement and is unlawful.

For example the Civil Service used to have an age bar of 28 years on applicants to Executive Officer grade. In Price v the Civil Service Commission Mrs Price argued that by imposing this condition the Civil Service was indirectly discriminating against women because more women than men are out of the labour market, particularly the full-time labour market because of family responsibilities. The Civil Service initially argued that while the condition was detrimental to women's opportunities it was justifiable and therefore lawful because of the need to create a balanced career structure within the Civil Service. The Industrial Tribunal found that the condition was not justifiable and therefore found against the Civil Service because the Civil Service had not looked at alternative methods of achieving a balanced career structure. The age bar is now 45 years.

Discrimination in Pay

The Equal Pay Act provides for equal pay for the same or broadly similar work or for work rated as equivalent under a job evaluation scheme. The Equal Pay Act requires that there be a man, past or present, with which the woman can compare herself, unless the claim is based on a job evaluation scheme.

The principle of equal pay has also been endorsed by Article 119 of the Treaty of Rome, of which Britain is a signatory, and the E.E.C. Directive on Equal Pay which is binding on the British Government. Both endorse the principle of equal pay for work of equal value and, recently, the European Court found that Britain was in breach of the European legislation because the Equal Pay Act did not provide for the principle for equal pay for work of equal value. In response, the Government is introducing an Order which has taken effect from January 1 1984 which has statutory authority and which endorses this principle. The Order will over-ride the limitation that there must be a man in the same or broadly similar work for the women to claim equal pay. This restriction has limited the effectiveness of the Equal Pay Act in achieving equal pay for women because of the nature of sex segregation in the workforce. The Order will place on employers a responsibility and give women the right to claim equal pay with men in totally different types of work, if the claim can establish that the work is of the same value in terms of effort, skill and decision-making. The concept of value is a highly complex one and is beyond the scope of this chapter to discuss in detail. Broadly speaking, the Order will require an assessment of jobs, in terms of pay and other contractual benefits based on value attached to different elements in each job. Traditionally more value has been attached to 'male' elements, such as strength, than 'female' elements such as dexterity.

Whereas direct discrimination focuses on assumed differences between groups of people, indirect discrimination is associated with an assumption of alikeness – a feeling that 'if they want to become like us they must behave like us'. This assumption or feeling constitutes the discriminations. Equality is sacrificed to equity.

Since the Sex Discrimination and Race Relations Acts were passed, case law, research and the experience of employers seeking to implement equal opportunity policies have further refined understanding of the process of discrimination in the workplace. It arises not only from the impact of specific actions and prejudices, but also from a failure to take into account the different social positions of women and men; minority and majority ethnic groups. It can also arise from a failure to translate effectively a policy statement into practice. Failure to do so amounts to discrimination by omission.

Thus, a truly equal opportunity employer would have to consider the impact of the following:

A practice of advertising all but a very few jobs on the assumption that they will be filled by a full-time worker essentially discriminates against women. Many more women than men find it difficult to work full-time, because a greater proportion of child-rearing responsibilities are currently assumed by women. Thus, women are more likely to wish to work part-time for at least a part of their working lives.

A practice of advertising jobs below a certain level internally first essentially discriminates against minority ethnic people if proportionately fewer minority ethnic people can comply with the requirement of already working for the organization than their presence in the local recruitment pool.

The absence of equal opportunity training and education programmes to assist managers and other decision-makers to identify the equal opportunity dimension of their every day practice and to respond to the needs of women and minority ethnic people is a further source of discrimination.

POSITIVE ACTION

Anti-discrimination measures alone are not enough to achieve equal opportunity in employment. They must be complemented by positive steps to redress the effect of past discrimination and to achieve change in discriminatory and stereotypical behaviour, arising from social attitudes, as the behaviour influences decisions about recruitment, selection, training, promotion, work organiz-ation etc. Discrimination endures in the attitudes, behaviour and practice of women and men long after regulations are neutralized.

Positive action can encompass continuous encouragement to evaluate and re-assess career opportunities; special training, in-cluding on-the-job training denied in the past; new career structures to enable movement into formerly unavailable positions and occupations; equal opportunity awareness and skills training for supervisors, managers, and interviewers.

The Sex Discrimination and Race Relations Acts specifically allow positive discrimination in the following ways:

1. Employers may encourage women and minority ethnic people to apply for work in areas in which they are under-represented by targeting advertising at the under-represented group and by providing them with special training.
2. Training agencies are allowed to orientate specifically training to women and minority ethnic people if during the previous 12 months no women or minority ethnic people (or very few) have been engaged in a particular kind of work.
3. Employers are allowed to provide training for existing em-ployees designed to encourage women and minority ethnic people into areas of work in which they are under-represented.

Positive Action is not a new concept. During both World Wars steps were taken to encourage women into non-traditional jobs and subsequently preference and retraining opportunities were given to war veterans. These well-tried and effective procedures should be applied to groups who have been seriously disadvantaged by systemic discrimination which is deeply embedded in our society.

A Positive Action Programme is based on the following principles:

1. Equal opportunity in employment is a matter of social justice.
2. There are two kinds of discrimination, direct and indirect, which must be eliminated if equal opportunity is to be achieved.
3. The fact of past discrimination, and its enduring legacy, means that redress action has to be taken in the form of positive steps to eradicate discrimination and remedial programmes for members of groups which have suffered discrimination.
4. Improvement in equal opportunity performance should be visible in the outcome of selection and promotion, and therefore

in the distribution of women and minority ethnic people in the workforce.

5. Positive action programmes should have specific goals and, where possible, numerical targets together with a timetable for their achievement. This enables the programme to be evaluated for its redistributive effect and its success in achieving the nominated targets.

Targets do not constitute quotas or proportionate hiring. They express the expectation that the desired numerical results will arise from the positive action programme. Targets should be realistic with regard to labour turnover and the availability of suitably qualified staff; but they should also be realistically ambitious to stimulate active and energetic implementation of the programme. Targets can be expressed in different ways. An employer may set a target of increasing the percentage of women in managerial positions by x per cent in 5 years or it might set itself the target of interviewing all its minority ethnic staff in 1 year to discuss career and training opportunities.

The setting of targets is a useful planning exercise. To determine a particular target, management must choose between competing goals and assess the effects of particular policies. It is an exercise in ordering priorities and assessing obstacles. Targets also provide the criteria for assessing the efficacy of genuine efforts and can stop the positive action programme being or appearing token.

PREPARING A POSITIVE ACTION PROGRAMME

The following guidelines are not intended as an aid to drawing up a positive action programme. They do not represent a 'fill in the blanks approach.' There is no substitute for careful analysis of an organization and the development of an individual plan to meet its own particular circumstance. It does not specifically relate to positive action for women. The model can also be used to develop a positive action programme for race equality and for people with disabilities.

Essentially, there are four stages to the development and implementation of a positive action initiative.

1. Outline policy preparation and communication.

2. A review of the sex profile of the company in relation to the impact of personnel policy and practice.
3. The identification of stategies to bring about change in the sex profile of the company and the establishment of objectives. This constitutes the positive action programme.
4. Implementation and evaluation of the positive action programme.

Stage 1. Policy Preparation and Communication

Aim: To establish commitment to equal employment opportunity and to involve personnel at all levels of the organization in the initiative.

It is important that the policy is endorsed at the highest levels of the organization, by the employer as well as workers' representatives. The statement should place responsibility for preventing discrimination and promoting equal opportunity on all management and employees. Responsibility for organizing the positive action effort should be invested in a senior manager with the authority to recommend and implement policy changes.

Co-operation and responsibility will be promoted if a positive action committee is established involving management, non-managerial staff and employee organizations. Women should be included in the Committee. Its function would be:

1. To advise and assist in the design and development of a positive action programme.
2. To monitor its impact and development.
3. To provide a forum for employees who wish to raise issues relating to the new policy and its implementation.

The establishment of an effective grievance procedure at this stage can promote acceptance of the programme by providing constructive assistance to employees with individual problems.

Checklist for drafting a policy statement on positive action
Such a statement should include:

A general statement of commitment to the eradication of discrimination and the promotion of equal opportunity.
A reminder of the provisions of the Sex Discrimination and Equal Pay Acts.

A brief outline of the proposed activities including their main areas of focus, i.e. recruitment, promotion, training, staff development and conditions of service.
Emphasis on results.
Name of the senior officer responsible.
A statement of the benefits of positive action in terms of the full use of human resources.
A clear statement of the responsibility of all those involved in personnel decisions and of managers to assist and co-operate with the development and implementation of the positive action programme, including their accountability for performance.
An invitation to employees to contribute ideas.

If established the policy statement should include the announcement of the Positive Action Committee and the Grievance Procedure.

The policy should be distributed to all employees and announced appropriately in all relevent internal and external literature, e.g. internal vacancy circulars, notification of vacancies through the careers service, job centres, and recruitment agencies, careers and induction literature, recruitment literature and job advertisements.

Stage 2. Review of the Sex Profile of the Company in Relation to the Impact of its Personnel Policies and Practices

Aim: To collect information which will aid design of the positive action programme and will also act as a benchmark against which progress can be measured and the efficacy of the programme assessed.

Collection of Statistical Data

First, take the categories in the organization and identify the proportion of women and men in each group. It is essential that the categories used are specific to the company and reflect its structure and identify the skill levels (skilled, semi-skilled, technical, clerical and professional) and occupations.

Second, analyse those categories which include women and men by salary, fringe benefits, (e.g. company cars, mortgages etc.), grade, access to training, qualifications, age, years of experience, marital status, children.

The aim of the analysis is to make comparisons. An obvious

comparison is the extent to which women and men of the same age with similar qualifications and years of service are receiving the same pay or are in jobs of equivalent status. The ease by which this sort of analysis can be done depends on the sophistication of the personnel records. Alternative ways of collecting this information are by:

1. *Headcount* – usually done through unit managers providing simple information, for example, sex by grade, job category, hours of work, e.g. full-time, part-time, shift work.
2. *Questionnaire* – directly to employees. Questionnaire can provide more complex information for comparison, e.g. age, qualifications, marital status, children, training, promotion and transfers. Without a computer, even a simple questionnaire can be very complex to analyse so it is often better to focus resources by looking in-depth at a few carefully chosen areas, e.g. a large and a small department, a female-populated area of work, a professional area of work.
3. *Personnel records* – may contain information on transfers, job evaluation appeals, reasons for resignation, etc.

Checklist for Collection of Statistical Data
Information of the organization's current workforce should be collected by sex for each of the following variables:

1. Major components of the organization, e.g. section, department.
2. Geographic locations.
3. Major job groups, e.g. managerial, technical.
4. Major occupational fields, e.g. administrative, engineering.
5. Pay.
6. Types of employment, e.g. full-time, part-time, shift, temporary.
7. Length of time in positions.
8. Resignations and transfers.
9. Qualifications.
10. Training.
11. Appeals.

Evaluation of Statistical Data
The purpose of this stage of the investigation is two-fold: to identify

any inadequacies in personnel policies and practices which discriminate against women and which can be changed to provide more equal opportunities; and to identify the specific disadvantages faced by women arising from organizational constraints and constraints imposed by society on women and men where redress action is needed to overcome the impact of past discrimination. This entails looking at each step of the employment process to see *where* and *why* women have difficulty in making progress.

For example, an analysis of employment patterns in the organization is highly likely to reveal women concentrated into 'support' positions such as secretarial and clerical jobs. The organization will have a policy that all job responsibilities be recorded in a job description. Research has revealed that a common feature of the job descriptions of employees in support functions is 'any other duties as directed'. In practice, this can mean anything from making the tea to very complex functions undertaken in lieu of the senior officer. In effect, this means that the organization and the employee may be unaware of the skills needed in the job and manifested by the job holder. This causes the organization problems in the induction and training of new staff, but it can also mean that the organization and the employee have difficulty recognizing the transferability of skills to new areas of work. To remedy this situation the organization might order the redefinition of job descriptions and personnel specifications. However, this action, although part of good equal opportunity practice, may not in itself encourage women in support positions to look at transferring their skills to a new area of work. Therefore the organization may decide to run career development workshops to encourage women to do so.

This stage of the investigation is best done by interview – both of managers (and other decision-makers) and of non-managerial staff. The intention is to look at what the organization says it does; the every-day practice and attitudes of managers and decision-makers, (e.g. interviewers) and to compare this with the experience and aspirations of all employees. The advantage of interviews is that the good practice of individuals can also be identified.

Below is a list of 'risk areas' under major aspects of personnel policy:
1. Job descriptions and personnel specifications:
   Are they free from sex bias,

Are they a simple and accurate description of the job and free from jargon,

Are the qualifications and experience required the essential minimum,

Is there a regular review of job descriptions and personnel specifications.

2. Recruitment and advertising:

Has recruitment literature been examined for sex bias in language and pictures,

Are boys' and girls' schools visited and are girls seen in mixed schools,

Do job adverts invite applications from women and men,

Are job adverts checked for unnecessary qualifications etc.,

Are all jobs advertised or is there a reliance on informal recruitment by word-of-mouth with the danger of like recruiting like.

3. Selection and appointment:

Are all questions asked at interviews and on application forms relevant to the position in question, e.g. are questions asked about family responsibilities,

Have qualification barriers and selection tests been assessed for sex bias and relevancy to the position in question,

In multiple recruitments are successful candidates placed in a non-discriminatory manner,

Have those involved in shortlisting and interviewing been trained.

4. Promotion and lateral transfer:

Do female-dominated occupations have career paths through a series of gradings representing a genuine increase in responsibility,

Does undue emphasis on seniority limit promotion opportunities for women,

Are there any programmes for inter-occupation transfer, late entry and retraining,

Are job descriptions for 'female' occupations less specific than for 'male' occupations, e.g. 'other duties as directed',

Do job descriptions for women omit duties done by women, either because the duties are considered to be 'favours' or because they are supposed to be done by a superior,

Do job descriptions for female occupation assign responsibility

'up-line' when these properly belong to the person performing the job,
Is there a staff appraisal scheme covering 'female' areas of work,
Are employees approached and offered careers counselling,
Does your organization require mobility as a pre-requisite for promotion,
Are exit interviews conducted to examine whether lack of progress is the cause of resignation.

5. Training and staff development:
Are training opportunities effectively publicised to all employees,
Are eligibility requirements for training courses minimal and essential,
Do nomination and screening procedures disadvantage women,
Are courses above a certain level only available on a residential basis,
Do the training courses fit the hours women work, e.g. part-time,
Does the organization run career-development workshops for women.

6. Conditions of service:
Are there equal female and male superannuation benefits,
Is flexible maternity and paternity leave provided,
Is short leave/emergency leave allowed for,
Do part-time employment opportunities exist in career positions,
Do women have equal pay. Is the work of female-dominated occupations undervalued in terms of pay. Is there equal pay for work of equal value – a concept about to be incorporated into our Equal Pay legislation.

Stage 3. The Identification of Strategies to Bring about Change in the Sex Profile of the Company and the Establishment of Objectives

Aim: to develop a plan of action to achieve change.
Strategies for the positive action programme should be both corrective and innovative. Corrective measures will remove the source of discrimination while innovative measure can seek to redress the effect of past discrimination and respond to the special

needs of women arising from past discrimination and their role in society.

Corrective: Abolish any unnecessary age bars.

Innovative: Develop a late-entry recruitment scheme.

It will be appropriate to adopt general measures to achieve a maximum use of human resources but some might be aimed at encouraging and expanding the opportunities of women.

General measure: Introduce an annual appraisal scheme for all employees.

Innovative measure: Introduce part-time career positions, perhaps through job-sharing.

The E.O.C. Code of Practice lists many measures which organizations should introduce as good practice. Below are some examples of initiatives taken by employers as part of their positive action programmes.

1. The appointment of an equal opportunity adviser.
2. The development of mature age-entry programmes and the general facilitation of re-entry into the workforce, for example, enabling the return of women and men who leave the organization's employ for domestic reasons for up to 5 years.
3. The maintenance of regular contact with education institutions in order to recruit women into non-traditional areas of work.
4. The development of a Code of Practice for interviews.
5. Equal Opportunity Awareness courses for all managers and decision-makers.
6. An equal opportunity input into induction courses of all staff.
7. The development of upward mobility programmes for low-level employees so that they have the opportunity to gain the skills necessary to compete for higher level positions, e.g. bridging courses.
8. The development of attachments schemes enabling women to try out non-traditional areas of work and gain some experience to enable them to compete for a job in that area.
9. The identification of career structures with limited opportunity, e.g. typing and secretarial work and where appropriate their consolidation with related career structures which provide more scope for advancement, e.g. administration.
10. The breaking-down of occupational stereotyping by, for example, requiring typing as a basic skill for occupations which make heavy use of typing facilities.

11. The establishment of elective permanent part-time employment opportunities in a broad range of jobs including those at the more senior level.
12. The institution of a child-care financial support scheme and/or creche facilities.
13. The establishment of numerical targets.

Stage 4. *Implementation and Evaluation*

Aim: To ensure that the programme is working and that progress is being made.

The implementation phase is the longest and most difficult phase of a positive action initiative. Negative responses to positive action can be expected, and strategies for dealing with this should be built into the positive action programme. For example:

1. There should be regular communication of the organization's commitment to the programme to all employees.
2. There should be regular consultation with the unions and, where appropriate, employees through workshop and general meetings.
3. Regular and continuous support and advice to employees at all levels in the organization, especially those whose day-to-day work practice is affected.
4. Regular reports to the workforce on the progress made, for example, through the company magazine, annual report or by special broadsheet.
5. The positive action programme should be institutionalized into the day-to-day practice of the organization and incorporated into the accountability line in the organization, for example, by including a specific equal opportunity responsibility in the duty statements of all managers and supervisors and the introduction of a means of appraising their performance.

8 Implementing equal opportunity
W. R. Brough

EQUAL OPPORTUNITY IN CONTEXT

Equal opportunity cannot be viewed, much less implemented, in isolation from a company's personnel policies, practices and beliefs. These factors may have created an environment within which equal opportunity is either fostered or hindered. At the same time, the actions available to further equal opportunity will vary according to the impact of policies and practices which may have established a situation highly favoured by employees of both sexes which would have to be traded off if certain 'positive actions' were to be taken.

This is certainly the case at IBM and the chart (Figure 8.1) shows the ingredients of the context into which equal opportunity falls. Whilst this context and comments on its relevance to equal opportunity are fully explained in the appendix, let me summarize them.

Firstly, there are those factors which create a good environment in which equal opportunity can grow – such as our basic belief of 'respect for the individual', being a single-status company and having a merit-based system of equal pay for equal work. Secondly, there are factors which allow us both to know what employees feel about equal opportunity – such as Opinion Surveys – and provide a channel through which concern about how the implementation of

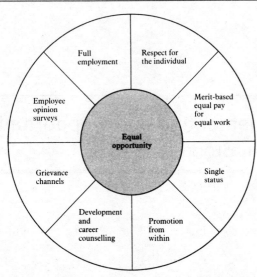

Figure 8.1 Equal opportunity in the context of IBM personnel policies and practices

equal opportunity affects them can be expressed. Then thirdly, there are those factors, highly regarded and cherished by our employees of both sexes, which give a greater balance of benefits to them than some of the so called 'positive actions' which they prevent. For example, promotion from within means that we could not recruit men or women into management positions. Our policy of full employment and the fact of low leaving rates generally – higher amongst women than amongst men – make changes to women's ratios to total employees a slow process.

Finally, there are the things we do to appraise, develop and counsel employees on their career progress. This process of performance management at once provides a framework within which equality of measurement, training and development can be fostered and an opportunity for employees to express their aims, desires and aspirations to their manager and obtain development and career counselling as a result.

INFLUENCING FACTORS

Thus, these several factors within the company environment both set a favourable climate for equal opportunity and provide some clues as to the speed with which change can take place and the factors which influence the actions we can take.

External Factors

There are many other influencing factors which warrant some comment, not least of which is the situation outside IBM. The position of women in society, the changes to their attitudes and aspirations, progress in other businesses, organizations and government, not to mention the attitudes of men, must all be taken into account in deciding how fast to move. Although change is not currently perceived as rapid, in the next five to ten years women will increasingly demand more career opportunities and a different quality of life. It has been said that such attitudes will increasingly be a matter of generation rather than of sex. There will be those, for example, whose life is more focussed on organized work, with men and women expressing the same demands for career and growth, and those whose life is less focussed on work with both men and women requiring a more flexible approach to the life-work cycle.

As these changes take place, so new demands will be placed on employers particularly in respect of the number of two-career families and the problems generated by them. These new demands are likely to manifest themselves in a number of ways:

1. The growing number of women in middle management positions and of young women with higher qualifications and expectations.
2. The end of the 'super-woman' syndrome: the one who got on in spite of everything.
3. The two-career family demands will no longer be perceived as a women's problem but rather one of all employees.

This situation will require companies to re-examine recruitment and relocation practices, to provide more flexible career paths and to arrange more flexible benefits. It will also require increasing care in the provision and the reality of equal opportunity. These changes are taking place already, albeit slowly, and therefore companies like IBM need to bear them and the rate of progress in mind when reviewing their policies and practices, and at least to anticipate the impact. What is more, women will form an increasing proportion of the available work force, and companies will have to make sure that they are attractive to women as places to work and thus avoid the loss of the resource and skills which women will eventually provide possibly in a greater degree than men. We need, therefore, to monitor the progress being made, to judge the rate at which change is likely to happen, and the impact this will have on IBM as a leading employer. Finally, in the context of outside influences, we are not only governed by the laws on equal opportunity and related areas, but wish to anticipate changes in the law and to that extent to be ahead of them.

Internal Factors

In addition to the policies and practices already discussed, there are other internal factors which influence the rate of progress in equal opportunity. In IBM, we have a low leaving rate amongst employees, but it is nonetheless somewhat higher for women than for men: this means we have to run fast in recruiting and promotion just to stay still in terms of the ratios of men and women employed and the numbers of women in higher level jobs. Recruitment is further influenced by the number of women applying, especially where technical qualifications are required. Promotion is influenced, of course, by the degree to which women wish to take advantage of it and prepare themselves accordingly. As you will see, actions can be taken to improve these situations, but not, I believe, dramatically, in the short term.

The visibility of equal opportunity within the company, the awareness that employees have of it and the desire that women have to take advantage of opportunities are all factors which have some bearing on progress. Furthermore, all companies develop their own characteristics and attitudes amongst both executive management and employees. We have to take into account the speed at which change will be acceptable both to employees and to management. The attitudes of both men and women are stereotyped to some degree and the view has been expressed that a large part of the problem with women's progress lies with the attitudes of women themselves. This raises the question of how much we should do to try to change attitudes – especially women's – and how much we should just ensure that no barriers to progress exist, leaving women to decide for themselves how and to what degree they wish to avail themselves of the opportunities afforded.

WHAT CANNOT BE DONE?

Before considering those areas in which I believe IBM can take actions I would like to review some areas where actions probably cannot be taken either because of legal constraints or because of constraints arising out of those policies and practices offering something which, on balance is more favourable to and more desired by employees of both sexes.

Quotas

Recruitment quotas are prohibited by law, and in any case would cut across the spirit of equal opportunity which, if it is to remain credible, must provide what the words imply. This also applies to the reserving of jobs for men or for women. On the one hand this could amount to preserving the very traditional roles which we are trying to break down. On the other hand it could cause resentment and resistance if someone of ability in either sex cannot get a job for which they may be better qualified than the person being put in it under the auspices of equal opportunity.

Change Ratios Quickly

On becoming a 'practitioner' in equal opportunity, I rapidly realized that there was a critical mass of employees where the ratio of male to female could not quickly be changed. In IBM we have around 15,000 employees of whom over 15 per cent are women: with relatively low recruitment and, as we have seen, women leaving at a rate faster than men, changing that 15 per cent is a longer term task. The same is true of smaller groups such as managers. We have over 2,000 managers, 3 per cent of whom are women: here again the impact of women leaving, or moving out of management coupled with negligible attrition amongst men managers, makes changing even that ratio a slow process.

This is not to say that change can be neither expected nor made: it is only to say that changing ratios will be slow and many of the actions taken can only have a longer-term impact. It is therefore reasonable to have goals for the longer term based on the company's policy, the constant re-inforcements of that policy, the increasing availability of suitably qualified women applicants, and the changes in women's personal career aspirations.

Manager Recruitment

It has from time to time been suggested that to help improve the ratio of women amongst managers, we should recruit highly qualified women into management from outside the company. This is both an interesting and tempting proposition, but one which would cut across our practice of promotion from within. Discussions with women in IBM indicate a clear preference for continuing our current practice, whilst men would see such a move as 'positive discrimination'. In either case, the cause of equal opportunity and the need constantly to be changing attitudes would hardly be enhanced.

Token Women

Another suggestion made is that we should deliberately promote some women to more senior professional and, especially, management positions in order to demonstrate our commitment to improving the ratios of women in these levels. Again, the evidence is that neither women nor men in the company would support such a move. IBM has a strong ethic of promotion and pay on merit: employees are imbued with this and enjoy its existence. Cutting across this would not be seen as furthering equal opportunity, and would run the risk of being counter-productive: that is to say, the chances of failure by the less qualified individual would be high and the consequences for fully qualified women somewhat undesirable. We have our fair share of chauvinists who would be confirmed in their long-held, but perhaps not articulated, opinion that women are 'unsuitable' for such jobs. It is better by far to spend our efforts and time in ensuring that those women who wish to can take full advantage of the development and opportunities available to them.

WHAT CAN BE DONE?

When first deciding how to meet the objectives of my job, I felt it necessary to get a clear personal understanding of my philosophy on equal opportunity, bearing in mind IBM's policy statements and existing practices. What I have written hitherto contains a large part of that philosophy, and this leads me naturally into the final phase of deciding which are the areas where activity could and should take place.

Monitor Progress

Here I refer to progress both inside and outside the company. The former is provided by cross-referencing our Personnel Data System, and analysing Opinion Surveys, whilst the latter is a question of reading the many publications available, attending and taking part in seminars and meetings and surveying other leading companies.

Influence Attitudes

I believe influencing attitudes is the most important activity I can undertake: in the final analysis no amount of policy statements, directions to management and monitoring of statistics will afford any benefits for women if the attitudes of both men and women are not changed. May I restate here my view that there is potentially more to be changed and much more to be gained in relation to attitudes held by women than those held by men. However, I firmly believe that having been made aware of the opportunity, some women wish to continue in a role more akin to that traditionally adopted by their sex than that advocated by the protaganists of women's movements, then they should be allowed to do so.

At the same time, the attitudes of managers need to be influenced so that any consciously or unconsciously held beliefs which are barriers to equal opportunity are gradually removed. I find an increasingly favourable attitude towards the recruitment and development of women which augurs well for continuing and accelerating progress.

Visibility and Awareness

Evidence from discussions and Opinion Surveys shows that many employees are unaware of the company's activities in equal opportunity and that this lack of visibility both hinders progress and provides an opportunity for misinformation. Awareness relates not only to knowing what the company is doing, but also to the need for employees to understand the law, the potential for indirect or unconscious discrimination and the effect this can have on both attitudes to and decision making about people.

Assist Career versus Family Problems

This area is somewhat more specific than the others, but is one which at the same time provides an opportunity for IBM to help women enjoy both a career and a family where that is desired and to retain valuable employees who might otherwise have to leave.

Provide Resources

It is unusual indeed, to find a company or organization 'employing' a manager full-time in the equal opportunity area. Yet it seems to me that this is an important way of ensuring both the development of a high degree of competence and the necessary amount of dedication. People with responsibility part-time are all too often distracted by their other commitments, but this can certainly be improved upon by the weight given to comparative job objectives, personnel management expectations and the allocation of time.

However, equal opportunity is clearly the responsibility of line management and not that of the personnel function. Unless line management understands this and is committed to it, then no amount of exhortation elsewhere will have the desired effect.

Women's Attitudes

I have already said that I have no wish, nor do I see any need, to dissuade women from the personal role they prefer and which gives them a satisfying quality of life. Rather, I am concerned with influencing the attitudes of those women who wish to pursue a more active career and yet are not ready or able to take more positive steps to fulfil their desires. From training and development programmes in which I have been involved, there is much evidence to show that once the sights of such women have been properly focussed then a more personally beneficial attitude to both work and life can be enjoyed.

Recruitment

This is the key vehicle through which the future composition of a workforce and management group will be changed. It therefore follows that any barriers to equal opportunity in selection must be removed or prevented from occurring, and the company seen by women as an attractive potential employer. In this respect, the content of recruitment literature, the composition of recruitment advertising and the attitudes of those involved in selection should all be given careful attention. Graduate recruitment is a key area in which to ensure equal opportunity in selection exists, since it is from this group that the future senior professionals and managers will grow.

Employee Development

All employees should have the development support they need in order both to achieve self-fulfilment and to be an improving resource for the company. Unfortunately, to make available such support does not necessarily guarantee that it will be used to its full advantage. Managers need to be aware of the different needs that women may have, whilst women need to be more prepared to take advantage of the benefits and potential which are available to them. I believe that many women do not take a strong enough position on the development programmes being offered to them and therefore managers assume that – as they always suspected – such women do not wish to do more.

Most of those involved in equal opportunity will probably find themselves comfortable with these areas of potential activity. These are not intended as an exclusive list: companies may wish to indulge in 'positive actions' of a different kind. I am reluctant to use this phrase, not so much because I disagree with its intentions, but more because I am concerned about its interpretation. Many employees to whom I have spoken believe that 'positive actions' are unlawful: in other words, they assume positive actions are synonymous with positive discrimination. I believe that any actions taken should be designed to help women to compete equally for opportunities and to prevent false barriers being placed in their way.

IBM PROGRAMMES

Having decided to appoint a full-time manager of equal opportunity programmes at the beginning of 1982, IBM put itself in a good position to take a more professional view of what needed to be done and the most appropriate ways in which to do it. But it is worth commenting that this job covered not only women but also disabled people and members of ethnic minority groups.

The major programmes for women can now be discussed in some detail.

Monitoring

The comprehensiveness of our Personnel Data System enables statistics on women's progress to be produced in a variety of forms. For example there are the obvious ones of percentage of total population, managers and professionals, as well as hires, leavers, reasons for leaving, level mix, performance rating, years of service, job types and so on. The key statistics are analysed every six months and are reviewed by the company's Executive Management together with recommendations for additional activities. Since these statistics have been measured for many years we can see the pattern of progress very clearly and can also compare ourselves to other IBM companies; and to leading British companies.

Equal Opportunity Dialogue

By 'dialogue' we infer an opportunity for a group of people to discuss the subject matter both with their peers and with representatives of management and executive groups. This particular 'dialogue' invited 18 women of various levels and jobs to come to St Hilda's College, Oxford for just over 2 days. The aims of the meeting were to raise women's self-awareness, to make them more aware of the opportunities available and to increase the visibility of equal opportunity programmes. Subjects covered included the progress being made outside IBM, the situation inside IBM, changing women's attitudes, how we identify and develop ability and an executive session covering the state of the business as well as dealing with questions on equal opportunity.

The programme was extremely successful and has been repeated. However, care needs to be taken in the number of 'women only' programmes and in explaining the reasons for them. Many of the women attending admitted to being highly sceptical before the meeting, but had their fears allayed by the end of it. However, the fact that this scepticism existed amongst women, and that suspicions of 'positive discrimination' exist amongst men, can only serve to underline the need for caution and careful explanation.

Equal Opportunity Seminars

The seminars usually last from 10 a.m. to 4 p.m. and are designed for audiences of both men and women. The aims are to raise the general level of awareness, to influence attitudes and to improve the visibility of equal opportunity. The content involves some present-ation of material on IBM's position and progress, but mostly takes the form of discussion on controversial but important issues concerning all aspects of equal opportunity. There is no shortage of discussion, but there is sometimes a shortage of men: it's a lot easier to get women along to such a seminar than it is men, even with the prospect of a free lunch.

Awareness Seminars

So far, these have been confined to personnel officers, and the content of the seminars concentrated on the need to be aware of the potential for discrimination. Personnel officers not only have themselves to consider: they frequently have to give advice to line management with whom they are aligned. Again there is a mixture of presentation and discussion, together with some group work, role plays etc. and a lot of emphasis is placed on awareness in the selection process. In 1982 we received about 26,000 applications for jobs: IBM therefore has to take care that equal treatment is given to all applicants irrespective of sex, marital status, race, ethnic origin, colour, nationality, age, religion or disability. Being more aware of the potential for discrimination, which is often unconscious, makes an important contribution to this end.

Manager Education

Management development courses are one of the key ways of

influencing managers' attitudes. Our main-stream courses contain various modules and case studies involving equal opportunity, whilst some divisional programmes have contained a more specific equal opportunity session. Giving a presentation on equal opportunity is, however, not nearly so likely to influence managers as is a more practical approach using in-basket exercises, role plays, and case studies. Fewer points may be made, but those made tend to have a greater effect. Another opportunity is afforded by annual Employee Relations/Industrial Relations updates provided by personnel groups and managers.

Departmental Meetings

Such meetings, whether of managers or run by managers for their subordinates, are an important way of raising the visibility of equal opportunity and of informing employees of the progress being made. Again, the material and approach used should be tailored to the audience – usually mixed – and the use of quizzes and case histories can bring the subject much more to life, and lead to a lot of healthy discussion and some influencing of attitudes.

Recruitment

There is a need to make the company an attractive place for people of both sexes to work in and, in particular, to attract a higher number of women applicants at the professional entry levels. We have been increasingly successful at doing this in our graduate recruitment programme: in 1981, for example, 33 per cent of our graduate intake were women in 1982; 41 per cent of the graduates recruited into our Marketing and Services Division were also women. There remains the difficulty of finding enough women applicants with engineering and similar degrees to enter our manufacturing and laboratory locations.

In trying to attract more women applicants, we have improved the appeal of our graduate recruitment brochure, and state in all our recruitment advertisements that we are 'an equal opportunity employer'. We avoid the use of 'all male' pictures or women depicted in so-called 'demeaning situations'.

Publications and Communications

In a company paying as much attention to communcations to employees as does IBM, there are many opportunities to publicize what we do in equal opportunity. The company newspaper is the channel most frequently used, but there are other opportunities such as Management Publications, an annual Employee Report and reference publications such as Employee Handbook and the Managers' Manual. By taking advantage of these publications, the visibility of equal opportunity is constantly enhanced as is employee awareness of what we are doing.

Opinion Surveys

These surveys take place every 18 months to 2 years on a divisional rather than a company-wide basis. Questions are asked about satisfaction with a wide range of aspects of employment, working conditions, policies and practices and management. There are questions specifically related to equal opportunity, which give a clear indication of how employees feel. The survey results can be analysed by men's and women's responses to each question. This analysis gives some interesting insights into the differences in motivations between the two sexes. Furthermore, employees have the opportunity to make written comments on any of the subjects addressed.

Following the surveys, each departmental manager is required to discuss the results for the department with his or her people and to present to them the actions to be taken in areas of low satisfaction, and review progress subsequently.

EO Surveys: Large Companies

In the middle of 1982, I conducted a survey of equal opportunity in 12 leading companies. The questions were kept simple in order to ensure that a reply was easy, and also that measurement could be made and conclusions drawn without too much difficulty. The ratios of women to total populations varied according to the nature of the business, and when it came to measuring 'managers' and 'professionals', it was difficult to get precise comparisons because of the different ways in which companies used these titles. It was clear, however, that there was very little activity by way of programmes, few special programmes of any kind for women only, and very little identification of women with potential. Equal opportunity was generally a responsibility conducted part-time alongside other activities.

Part-time Work

Since June 1981, IBM has been running an experiment which allows up to 20 women each year to enter into part-time work before returning full-time no later than 3 years after their confinement. This experiment was undertaken to provide women with another alternative after maternity leave, to help with the growing desire to have both a career and a family, to enable IBM to retain valuable employees in whom a considerable investment had been made, and to contribute to equal opportunity in careers and development.

So far the scheme has been successful in terms of those objectives which can be measured to date, but ultimate success can only be measured in terms of the number of women returning full-time after their 3 years or less of part-time work. This will not be possible before the end of 1984.

Women's Development

The subject of 'women only' training courses remains a controversial one. Generally, we would see most development taking place on the wide range of manager and non-manager training programmes provided for both men and women. However, we have experimented with some 'women only' training, and it does seem that it has a part to play. A small number of women employees have attended short courses outside IBM and found them beneficial. Others have attended internal courses, sometimes run internationally, which have also been highly rated by the participants. From these experiments it does seem probable that at least some women can have their attitudes changed significantly and positively enough to make them a greater asset to the company, more effectively able to compete for opportunities and more able to take advantage of the internal development programmes.

CONCLUSION

In a business and social world where prejudice or discrimination is based on generalized assumptions developed from our background and experience, influencing attitudes in a positive way is the most important contribution I feel people doing my job can make in equal opportunity. This might be a slow process, but I believe it will gather momentum the more attitudes become changed. In IBM, we are committed to providing equal opportunity in all aspects of selection and employment. The programmes we have in place are designed both to support that commitment and to assist the pace of change within the context of what is acceptable to and desired by the majority of our employees.

APPENDIX: THE IBM CONTEXT

The chart (Figure 8.1) shows how equal opportunity fits into the IBM personnel context, but the other sections also have some relevance to equal opportunity.

Equal Pay and Benefits

For many years, IBM has had a system of equal pay irrespective of sex. The system is based on the job level and the quality of performance in that job. The job levels are developed by Job Evaluation, with a salary range available for each job level. An employee's position in the salary range is determined by the length of time in that level and the measurement of performance in carrying out responsibilities. The system is therefore merit-based and, in this respect, the amount paid to each individual – even with similar service – may vary. Individuals can ask their manager to explain where they are in the range and should be able to understand why. All pay rises have to be signed off by a manager's manager, with personnel keeping a watching brief for fairness. Equality also applies to benefits, and an interesting example is to be found in our recently revised pension plan which provides retirement for both men and women between 60 and 63.

Full Employment

This practice means that in the event of a job or jobs disappearing, for whatever reason, IBM will seek every opportunity to redeploy the individual or individuals affected. This may involve training, relocation or transfer, but the principle aim is to keep the individuals employed as long as performance is satisfactory, rather than make them redundant. Again, this applies regardless of sex.

Promotion from Within

Since managers or higher-level professionals, whether men or women, are promoted from within, it is critical that IBM does a very good job not only in selecting its employees but also in developing them to take more responsibility as opportunities arise. From time to time it has been suggested that we should recruit some women with MBAs directly into management: apart from the fact that this would be viewed as discriminatory and would also cut across the spirit of equal opportunity, both male and female employees would find such actions less attractive than promotion from within.

Single Status

This is a close relation of equal opportunity and helps a sense of equality within the company. By single status, we mean not only specific things such as having only one cafeteria or car park irrespective of status in the company, but also it relates to the broader aspect of the treatment given to all employees in all our employee practices.

Grievance Channels

Should any employee feel that he or she has been wrongly treated, then that situation can be escalated to the manager's manager. This is where most problems are resolved. But should the employee desire it, then the appeal can be made to any higher level of management chosen by the employee. We call this practice 'The Open Door'. Should an employee wish to raise an issue anonymously, then this can be done through the 'Speak Up!' programme where concerns or requests for information or help are sent via a third party who preserves the anonymity of the writer. Both procedures are well used and are generally seen as appropriate to their purpose. Should anyone feel discriminated against or see there are barriers to his or her equality of opportunity therefore, suitable channels through which to pursue the concern. Managers know that this opportunity for their actions to be challenged or appealed against is a key part of our personnel practices.

Opinion Surveys

These surveys seek employees' opinions about their degree of satisfaction with a wide range of subjects relating to employment, working conditions and management. One of the subjects addressed is equal opportunity. This gives the company a barometer of feeling on this as on other subjects and enables us to make plans accordingly. The survey results can also be analysed so that men's and women's responses can be compared in all cases giving valuable information upon which to base future actions and provide appropriate forms of motivation.

Performance, Appraisal and Development

Each employee should have at least an annual appraisal of performance and a review of the development required both in the light of that performance and career opportunities. This appraisal of performance subsequently influences both pay and prospects and is seen by the employee and signed as a result. The development and career discussions offer all employees an opportunity to state what their aspirations are, and to have them recorded, whilst the employee's manager gives his or her views on these aspirations and together they work out a development programme. I believe this is a critical opportunity for women; if they wish to make progress then this review is the point at which they should be saying so and at which they should be sure they are happy about the development plans being agreed.

Respect for the Individual

This is one of the basic beliefs upon which the IBM Company was founded, and every manager knows that this must pervade all his dealings with subordinates. However, I believe that having and implementing this basic belief in IBM is a tremendous asset in fostering equal opportunity within the company and ensuring that manager's attitudes to their subordinates are in line with the company's policy.

9 Policies for women managers in the 1980s: what corporate America is doing to foster career development and organizational commitment
Sue Greenfeld and
Susan Rawson Zacur

Changes in societal conditions have fostered an influx of women into the United States' paid workforce. Seven out of ten women work out of economic necessity as the head of a household or as a major contributor to family income. Women are becoming more career-oriented in their employment outlook due to higher educational achievement and the realization of a longer work-life expectancy. Women now outnumber men enrolled in U.S. colleges and universities. The retirement age has been raised to 70 while family size is decreasing. These societal factors imply that women, especially those with strong educational investments, will probably be working 30 to 50 years outside the home. Traditional occupational fields for women such as education, social work and nursing are experiencing contraction of opportunities, while the business and service sectors have been expanding their need for managers with strong communication skills. Legal requirements for equality of opportunity in selection, promotion and compensation have caused employers to open both entry-level positions and promotional pathways in the management ranks to women and minorities. Thus, societal conditions are causing women in America to seek managerial opportunities at a time when employers are willing to offer such placement.

In the past twenty years, the above-mentioned antecedents have had a direct and dramatic impact on corporate programs and policies for developing the American woman manager. There are now more women managers, in absolute number, and a greater representation of women throughout the corporation than ever before in U.S. history. Some employing organizations are increasingly supportive in providing a climate conducive to developing a woman's career potential and it is these corporate role models that will be highlighted in this chapter.

Our focus is upon how the American woman manager has progressed in the past twenty years since the passage of the Civil Rights Act of 1964 which, in Title VII, prohibits discrimination in employment based on sex as well as race, color, religion or national origin (See Table 9.1). In particular, we will be addressing some relevant initiatives in the areas of (1) affirmative action, which includes recruitment, development and promotion of women and (2) employment policies, which include flexible work scheduling, relocation, maternity benefits, and child care. U.S. corporations are taking these actions to help foster the development and retention of the American woman manager. In particular, we will highlight some of the exciting and worthwhile steps U.S. companies have initiated for the 2.2 million American female managers.

AFFIRMATIVE ACTION

Affirmative Action is a set of specific steps designed to foster greater employment and promotional opportunities for classes protected by law. These steps are combined into a programme, including analysis of the company's present workforce, comparison of that workforce with the labour market in terms of demographics, and an outline of actions that will be taken to increase opportunities for women and/or minorities according to a reasonable timetable. Affirmative action programmes are carried out by companies in the U.S.A. for one of three reasons: (1) a firm has been found guilty in court of some form of employment discrimination and has therefore been ordered to create and carry out an affirmative action plan to hire and promote qualified members of the minority class to

Table 9.1   Major U.S. Laws or Orders Affecting Female Employees

Title	
Equal Pay Act, 1963	Requires same pay for men and women doing equal work requiring equal skill and responsibility; permits wage differentials based on bona fide seniority merit system. As of July 1, 1972, *the protection was extended to executive, administrative*, and *professional employees*. As of May 1, 1974 the act was extended to employees of Federal, State and Local governments.
Title VII of the Civil Rights Act, 1964, as amended by the Equal Employment Opportunity Act, 1972	Prohibits discrimination based on sex, as well as on race, colour, religion and national origin. Bars hiring based on stereotyped characterization of sexes.
Executive Order 11246 effective Oct. 14, 1968	Prohibits discrimination based on sex by Federal contractors or sub-contractors whose contracts exceed $10,000; contractors must take affirmative action in recruitment, hiring, selection or training.
Title VII of the Civil Rights Act, 1974, as amended by the Pregnancy Disability Act, 1978	Prohibits discrimination on the basis of pregnancy, childbirth or related medical conditions in hiring, promotion, suspension, discharge or in any other term or condition of employment.

compensate for past discrimination within the company; (2) a company is a federal government contractor and is therefore required to have an affirmative action plan by Executive Order or (3) an organization considers affirmative action to be part of its social responsibility and voluntarily enacts a plan for the recruitment and promotion of women and minorities at all levels of the organization. American Telephone and Telegraph, U.S.A.'s largest utility company, fits into the first category based upon an out-of-court settlement; General Electric, Westinghouse Corporation, Lockheed and other major defence contractors fall into the second category while Levi Strauss, America's largest clothes manufacturer, exemplifies the third. Regardless of why firms have affirmative action plans, the results are dramatic (Table 9.2). Clearly, affirmative action has made a difference. The number of women managers has started to reach beyond the token stage as indicated by a 1980 executive search study which estimated the proportion of women officers at entry level management at 28 per cent, middle level 8.8 per cent and top level 1.5 per cent (Allen, 1980). Corporate policies on recruitment, development and promotion have been effective in carrying out affirmative action goals.

Table 9.2

Company	Estimated percentage increase in women managers since the 1970s
1. American Express Co.	110
2. AT&T	473
3. Connecticut General	183
4. Continental Illinois	294
5. Control Data	1,725
6. Digital Equipment	10,000
7. Equitable Life	540
8. Hewlett Packard	236
9. Honeywell	157
10. IBM	790
11. Johnson & Johnson	148
12. Quaker Oats	97

Adapted from O'Toole (1982) and Scholl (1983).

Recruitment and Development

In the area of recruitment, companies have reached out to women graduates of business schools by on-campus recruitment and by advertising focussed upon women. On-campus recruitment has targeted women's colleges and women students. On-campus recruiters have been selected for their ability to relate positively to female candidates and have been trained in the legalities of employment interviewing so as to present a favourable company impression. Advertisements in business and women's publications have been carefully designed to provide visual images of women in professional jobs. The copy is unbiased and the words 'Equal Opportunity Employer' are prominently displayed. However, the inclusion of female role models along with male and minority representatives has helped women feel more comfortable about employment with a firm presenting such an image.

Development efforts have been expanded as companies have continued to practice a promotion-from-within approach to filling managerial positions. In order to provide access for women, for example, Connecticut General Corporation, a major financial and life insurance institution, opened its management development programme to women in the early 1970s. Women began rotational job assignments throughout the insurance company resulting in increased knowledge, exposure and promotional opportunities (O'Toole, 1982). Continental Illinois Corporation, parent company for the tenth largest U.S. bank, revamped its management training program in 1975 allowing B.A.s the same access as M.B.A.'s. The result was a dramatic increase in the enrollment of women, a greater diversity of managerial backgrounds and corporate flexibility that has made the bank a top performer in its industry (O'Toole, 1982).

In addition to greater access to management training, programme content has been directed at women. American Express Company, one of the world's largest travel card and traveller's cheque organizations, provides a six-month evening course for its women. Digital Equipment Corporation, a high-technology computer company, offers women a career leadership-development programme to facilitate personal career goal-setting. Digital also provides seminars for men and women wherein work and gender role issues can be explored through a male/female awareness workshop (O'Toole, 1982).

A further development effort that has achieved positive results is the recognition and encouragement of developing women managers through the use of support groups. The Women's Council at CBS, Inc., one of three major U.S. broadcasting companies, has presented concerns to management resulting in greater dissemination of job opportunities through posting (Scholl, 1983). At the Equitable Life Assurance Society of the United States, an insurance institution, a rotating panel of women meet with top management on a regular basis to discuss and advise on women's issues with the company (O'Toole, 1982).

Gannett Company, publisher of a national daily newspaper, *USA Today* is part of an industry that has chiefly been run via an Old Boy's network. Yet, Gannett is ahead of industry averages in the placement of women at all levels in the organization. The women at Gannett found themselves entering sub-societies organized by men when they entered the management ranks. In order to help one another and exchange information, some women organized a network support group. The Gannett corporation responded by hiring a consultant to work with the women's network in order to listen to the group's concerns and foster improved communications. Although the network eventually disbanded, more women were promoted and they continued to learn about and adapt to corporate culture with the comfort of knowing that they were not alone (Bernikow, 1983).

Wall Street Professional Women meet in corporate dining rooms on a monthly basis to discuss stocks as well as day care, domestic help or ideas on combining a career and motherhood. This working mother's group is a committee of the professional Financial Women's Association whose 400 members earn well over $50,000 a year as investment analysts, portfolio managers or commercial bankers in New York City (Witty, 1981). Although sponsored by a professional organization, company support for the Women's group via provision of a meeting place during the middle of a work day serves as recognition of the value of the support activity. Thus, the support approach to developing women managers is being employed with success in progressive firms.

Promotion

The promotion of women is clearly facilitated by the development and support efforts described above. In addition, companies have worked to devise objective performance appraisal systems that can give developmental feedback while pinpointing women with growth potential. General Mills, a $2 billion-a-year food processor, monitors the progress of women and minorities through an ongoing series of internal audits (O'Toole, 1982). The 3M Company, a world leader in cellophane tape and 84,000 other products, has also developed an extensive personnel review system designed to give feedback and career development support (Scholl, 1983).

To foster promotional opportunities, some companies encourage mentoring or sponsoring relationships between employees. For example at Honeywell, a high technology company, promising young women and minorities are paired with senior executives who act as coaches and sponsors when promotional opportunities occur. Security Pacific Corporation, a West coast-based financial institution, offers an Advanced Opportunity Programme wherein senior managers offer career and political advice to up-and-coming women and men (O'Toole, 1982). 3M calls its effort the High-Potential Employee identification programme. Managers present a tracking plan for the selected employee which is reviewed by an executive resources committee. This employee's progress is then tracked within the company to be sure progress is made and the career does not become stalled due to mishandling by supervisory personnel.

Each of the above actions has been invaluable for helping women to attain managerial rank. Such career development efforts reinforce the positive feeling that the woman manager has for her company, and thus, enhances her organizational commitment to her employer. Equally important, there are corporate policies supportive of a female manager once she has attained her new position. These policies, which we address next, demonstrate a firm's additional sensitivity to employees' needs.

EMPLOYMENT POLICIES

Flexible Working Scheduling

In 1981, the U.S.A. held a national meeting designated the 'White House Conference on the Family.' At this meeting, Congressional representatives and experts gathered to discuss the relevant issues facing the American Family. Significantly, its number one recommendation was that 'business initiate family-oriented personnel practices' (McCrosky, 1982). Obviously, such a recommendation would materially affect the woman professional who has to balance a high-powered career with home life. High on the list of policies frequently mentioned in this area is flexible work scheduling composed of flexitime (or flextime) and flexplace (allowing a woman to work at home).* A *Business Week* survey in 1982 suggested that an increasing number of corporations are turning to flextime as companies realize they need to accommodate the special needs of married women managers 'or lose them'.

Users of flextime report numerous advantages including flexibility in getting to work, non-rush hour commuting and the ability to handle child-care arrangements with less hassle. For example, New York-based Metropolitan Life Company, the second largest life insurance company in the U.S., started its flextime system in 1975 and continues to use such scheduling because of reduced tardiness and the employee's ability to handle childcare with greater ease. Women are the major users of flextime at Metropolitan Life. (Horstmann, 1982). A 1981 Catalyst Report entitled *Corporations and Two Career-Families: Directions for the Future* surveyed 374 companies of which 37 per cent reported having flexible working hours. Yet, 73 per cent of the companies favoured having such a practice (Catalyst, 1981).

Women managers appreciate and use flexible work schedules. 'I wouldn't be able to work without flexible hours' reports a female manager of personnel systems and research at Continental Illinois Bank and Trust in Chicago. But, she first had to quit Continental Illinois, obtain another job at Bell & Howell where such adjustments were made and returned to Continental only after it changed its policy and allowed flextime (Business Week, 1981). At Equitable Life Assurance Society, employees in the Career Part-time (CP-T) programme are eligible for all benefits, but must work at least a 50 per cent schedule. Salary and vacation time are prorated. The most frequent users of the programme have been technical and clerical personnel but there have also been some individuals in the organization near vice-presidential rank who have been in the CP-T Programme (Lund, 1982).

Complementing flextime is the newer concept of 'flexplace' which allows for work to be completed in the home. One leader in this field

*Flextime has been defined as a band of time (usually 7–9am or 3–5pm) in which an employee can arrange to arrive or leave work, provided the employee works the expected 7½ or 8 hours for that day.

is Control Data Corporation, a Minneapolis-based computer company, which has a flexplace policy called HOMEWORK developed originally to help employees who were disabled to get back to work as soon as possible. This concept has now been expanded to include other workers. Employees are considered for remote employment after working in-house for a specified period of time. This is particularly helpful to a professional who wants to stay at home after childbirth and retain her professional career path.

Another organization which has been cited for a willingness to use flexplace is New York Telephone. This employer allowed a couple, husband and wife were product managers for the company, to work some of the time at home (Shreve, 1982). By allowing work at home, the employer is helping the woman employee to balance her professional career development needs with her family life needs.

Relocation

Another issue with implications for women managers is company policy on relocation and whether or not the company has a lenient attitude toward hiring or aiding in placement of the spouse of the transferred employee. On the way to the top, the woman's career will need to 'grow', often with the added responsibilities of a corporate position in another geographic location. Corporations have long had established policies on relocation, but these normally included moving and living expenses without regard for the livelihood of the employee's spouse. The corporation that sees its responsibility as helping the employee and her spouse find appropriate career placement will attract and retain qualified women managers.

In the previously cited Catalyst study, one-quarter of the 815 dual-career couples moved for the wife's career. One-half of this group received some kind of assistance. The most frequently mentioned service was, of course, moving expenses (42.5 per cent) followed by locating a suitable community (25.7 per cent), purchasing a home (22.8 per cent), counselling in school (12 per cent) and finally, finding a job for her husband (7.8 per cent) (Catalyst, 1981). Aluminium Company of America, a $4.7 billion metals and mining company, recently formed a task force whose agenda includes finding out how to facilitate spouse employment after a relocation (Hunter, 1982). General Electric (GE), a Connecticut-based home and industrial appliance maker, has a dual-career programme tailored to executives with working spouses. GE is committed to helping the employee's husband find a job in a new location (Scholl, 1983).

The most beneficial policy for relocating the dual-career couple is when the employer has a liberal philosophy of hiring both the husband and the wife as a package. While many organizations do have strict anti-nepotism policies, there are organizations who have taken a very enlightened view. In an informal survey of twelve Baltimore-area companies, three corporations revealed a very supportive stance in their personnel hiring policy: Bendix, an aerospace and auto-parts manufacturer, Bethlehem Steel and Westinghouse. All three will hire husband-wife teams provided that one spouse does not supervise the other. Even more progressive, E. F. Hutton, a stock brokerage firm, has indicated a willingness to hire a husband-wife team to share a job. Thus, these corporate leaders are demonstrating their sensitivity to the relocation issue.

Maternity

Title VII of the Civil Rights Act of 1964 was amended in 1978 to broaden the definition of sex discrimination to encompass pregnancy, childbirth, or related medical conditions.* The Pregnancy Disability Amendment makes it an unfair employment practice to discriminate on the basis of pregnancy, childbirth or related medical conditions in hiring, promotion, suspension, discharge or in any other term or condition of employment. In practice, this means that (1) a U.S. employer cannot require women to take leave arbitrarily set at a certain time in the pregnancy rather than based upon inability to work; and (2) the employer cannot fail to grant full re-instatement rights to women on leave for pregnancy-related reasons. Title VII prohibits discriminatory treatment, but it does not require employers to treat pregnant employees in any particular manner with respect to hiring, permitting them to continue working, providing sick leave, furnishing medical and hospital benefits, providing disability benefits or any other matter. The law simply requires that pregnant women be treated the same as other employees on the basis of their ability or inability to work (Trotter,

*PL 95–555 Sec. 1, 92. Stat. 2076, 42, U.S.C. Sec. 200 (e) (K).

Zacur and Gatewood, 1982). Of interest then, are the policies that various U.S. companies have promulgated in order to deal with pregnancy and maternity among women managers.

In general, companies now let women work as long as they choose during their pregnancy. Although certain work assignments may be considered hazardous due to exposure to unsafe conditions, it is generally left to the woman and her physician to decide what she can do. Atlantic Richfield Company of Los Angeles, an oil producer and refiner, and most major employers now follow this policy.

Maternity leave ranges from six weeks off with pay at Kraft, Inc. of Glenview Illinois, a food processor, to six month's leave with 60–100 per cent of salary at Aetna Life and Casualty Company of Hartford, Connecticut (Business Week, 1983). Leave policies may be made more flexible to suit the individual manager and her work schedule by allowing for use of a computer terminal and/or writing time at home in the case of financial managers and editors or communications experts, respectively. Equitable Life Assurance Society of the United States offers this option through the previously mentioned Career Part-Time Program, while Citibank, a financial institution, and Merck and Company, a $2.4 billion pharmaceutical and ethical drug company, offer similar options (Lund, 1982).

Day Care

Once pregnancy and post-partum leave are behind her, the woman manager in the United States is faced with the crucial issue of finding acceptable, professional care for her child or children while she is at work. In the past, women managers sought live-in or all-day help by a housekeeper due to the fact that other day-care options were non-existent or inadequate. Companies are now beginning to offer working mothers new alternatives. From the tax point of view it is in the corporation's best interest to do so.*

Connecticut General Corporation has a day-care centre at its headquarters in Bloomfield, Connecticut (O'Toole, 1982), as does Corning Glass Works in Corning, New York and PCA Inter-

*Under the Economic Recovery Tax Act, 1981, U.S. employers can deduct the cost of child care benefits they offer. These include on-site day care, direct payments for outside day-care centre or re-imbursement for cost of housekeepers and baby-sitters whose services are employment-related.

national Inc. in Matthews, North Carolina (Fooner, 1982). Re-modelling an unused facility and then leasing it to a day-care company provided the mechanism for this valuable fringe benefit. Intermedics in Freeport, Texas offers a company-run day-care centre and has been able to show significant decreases in job turnover and absenteeism since its inception (Department of Labor, 1982).

Companies such as Manufacturers Life, Wang Laboratories Inc., a computer and word-processing company, and Lormey Engineering Company, a Texas-based mechanical and electronic engineering firm, subsidize or invest in child care. (Fooner, 1982). Honeywell, Inc., an advanced-technology company in Minneapolis, Minnesota has created a new position, Working Parents Resource Co-ordinator, to help employees find useful resources and to guide company policy (Fooner, 1982). Some firms subscribe to a computerized location service that can help parents find appropriate help. In Baltimore, the Maryland Committee for Children runs such a service for a fee of $5.00 per person (The Baltimore Sun, 1983).

Consequently, the employment policies that help women managers help all women workers. Employers have created and/or expanded these policies only in recent years although most have employed women at lower organizational levels for as long as they have been in business. The impetus for these policies has come from an interest in attracting and retaining qualified women managers to meet affirmative action goals as well as to foster the organizational effectiveness that results from the employment of capable personnel.

In this chapter, we have reviewed affirmative action efforts in the recruitment, development and promotion of women. We have also examined employment policies such as flexible work scheduling, relocation, maternity and child care benefits as they help companies to retain qualified women. These policies foster organizational commitment while the affirmative action efforts promote career development. Women managers are today considered a valuable human resource and enlightened employers are taking appropriate actions to encourage active career involvement. These industry leaders are setting examples that their counterparts will inevitably follow as the competition for talent grows stronger with renewed economic growth in traditional sectors and increasing expansion in high-growth sectors. Women managers are clearly a force to be reckoned with in the United States today.

REFERENCES

Allen, F. 'Women Managers Get Paid Far Less Than Males, Despite Career Gains', *Wall Street Journal*, 7 October 1980, 35.

Bernikow, L. 'The Paper Tiger', *Savvy*, June 1983, **4**, 6, 38–43, 84–5.

Business Week, 'Working Around Motherhood', 24 May 1982, 188.

Business Week, 'When the Mother-to-be is an Executive', 11 April, 1983, 128.

Catalyst: Career and Family Center. *Corporations and Two-Career Families: Directions for the Future*, A report based on the findings of two national surveys (Catalyst: New York, 1981).

Fooner, A. 'Who's Minding the Kids', *Working Woman*, May 1982, 99.

Horstmann, V. 'Beyond Nine to Five', *Working Woman*, May 1982, 97–8.

Hunter, W. 'On the Job: Relocation', *Working Woman*, February 1982, 16–18.

Lund, S. 'Kids and Careers', *Working Woman*, July 1982, 54, 56–8.

McCrosky, J. 'Work and Families: What is the Employer's Responsibility', *Personnel Journal*, January 1982, 30–8.

O'Toole, P. 'The Savvy Sixteen', *Savvy*, May 1982, **3**, 5, 41–4.

Scholl, J. 'Savvy Corporations of the Year', *Savvy*, June 1983, **4**, 6, 30–7.

Shreve, A. 'Careers and the Lure of Motherhood', *The N.Y. Times Magazine*, 21 November 1982, 38–43, 46, 48, 50, 56.

The Baltimore Sun, 21 April 1983, E1.

Trotter, R., Zacur, S. R. and Gatewood, W. 'The Pregnancy Disability Amendment: What the Law Provides – Part I', *Personnel Administrator*, February 1982, 53.

U.S. Department of Labor Women's Bureau. *Employers and Child Care: Establishing Service through the Work Place*. (Washington, D.C., 1982), 5.

Witty, M. 'Financial Women and Children', *Working Woman*, September 1981, 77–9.

Useful information for women in management

1. Women in Training News. This provides a quarterly newsletter for women in management. Contact Ann Cooke, Group Co-ordinator, C/o Department of Management Studies, Gloucestershire College of Arts & Technology, Oxstalls Lane, Gloucester GL2 9HW.
2. Women in Management: an organization looking at the problems of women in administrative and management roles. Contact 4 Mapledale Avenue, Croydon CR0 5TA.
3. Women in Engineering. Contact Women's Engineering Society, 25 Foubert's Place, London W1V 2AL.
4. Equal Opportunities Commission. Contact Mr Wilf Knowles, Equal Opportunities Commission, Overseas House, Quay Street, Manchester.
5. Women of Europe, The Commission of the European Communities, 200 Rue de la Loi, 1049 Brussels.
6. The 300 group, This group looks at women in political life. Contact the 300 Group, Nettlebed, Oxfordshire.
7. Training Opportunities for Women. Training Services Division, Manpower Services Commission, Moorfoot, Sheffield.
8. Women at Work Unit, Department of Management Sciences, U.M.I.S.T., P.O. Box 88, Manchester. Contact Professor Cary L. Cooper.

Index